Digital Mixology

Crafting the Perfect Blend of Data, Technology, and Innovation

Chris Airey

Technics Publications
SEDONA, ARIZONA

TECHNICS PUBLICATIONS

115 Linda Vista, Sedona, AZ 86336 USA
https://www.TechnicsPub.com

Edited by Steve Hoberman
Cover design by Lorena Molinari

First Printing 2025

ISBN, print ed.   9781634627375
ISBN, Kindle ed.   9781634627412
ISBN, PDF ed.   9781634627429

Library of Congress Control Number: 2025935923

Contents

Foreword by Chris Potts _____1

Dedication_____3

Chapter 1: What Good Looks Like _____5
The Outside-In Approach_____15
The Four Levels of Outside-In _____19
Outside-In vs. Inside-Out_____21
You Don't Have the Silver Bullet (That's Okay!) _____27
The Danger of Your Biases _____32
The Biggest Mistake That Leaders Make _____41
Find Your Digital Mixologist_____50
Test and Learn _____56

Chapter 2: The Power of Customer Confidence _____57
Confidence Attracts Customers_____61
Unpacking Your Self-Confidence_____70
Your Customers Want the Perfect Cocktail _____76

Chapter 3: Delivering Digital and Creating Productive Change __79
The Four Easy Steps_____83
The Journey to Reflective Competence_____88
Discovering the Knowns and Unknowns _____96
The Service Design Philosophy_____103
Service Design and Your People_____111
Your Organization Is a Living Organism _____116
Agile is of course dead? _____124
Creating Collective Ambition—The Glue and the Grease _____124
Cost vs. Capability_____129
It's Time to Create Magic_____131

Chapter 4: The Two Bits of Magic _____ 133
  What Does Quality Mean? _____ 135
  Mixologists Help Realize Quality of Ambition _____ 137
  You're Living in a VUCA World _____ 139
  The New VUCA World _____ 141
  Creating Flow in Your Organization _____ 145
  The Defense Mechanisms That Hamper Ambition _____ 157
  The Keys to Mixology _____ 167

Chapter 5: Your People Are Your Power _____ 171
  It's Not Hard _____ 173
  Customer Engagement Pays Off _____ 177
  The Bits That Organizations Miss—People and Processes _____ 180
  Confronting Common Organizational Blockers to "Good Digital" _ 185
  Help Your People to Perform _____ 192

Chapter 6: It's Time to Create Change _____ 193
  The Organization Laws of Physics _____ 195
  The Psychological Inertia Problem _____ 201
  The Five Steps for Creating Change (So You Can Deliver Value) 207
  Organize for Success _____ 217
  Getting Some Quick Wins _____ 224
  It's Time to Enjoy Digital _____ 229

Helpful Resources _____ 231

Index _____ 235

Foreword by Chris Potts

Every enterprise builds up inertia from the moment that it's created. The cumulative effect of all the rational and not-so-rational decisions people have made gives us an enterprise that, naturally, allows changes that align with its existing speed and direction of travel and resists all those that might knock it off course.

Our enterprise's inertia can be most obviously exposed when we mix it with innovation and find out what happens. Time, and our outcomes, will tell which ends-up disrupting the other.

Innovations that work create the "unbalanced force" that permanently alters our enterprise's destiny. The ones that don't may create the illusion of change, but our enterprise is still - if we look carefully - the same. Our challenge is to successfully invert the inevitability suggested in Jean-Baptiste Alphonse Karr's epigram, *"Plus ça change"* which translates to... the more our enterprise changes, the more it actually does.

In *Digital Mixology*, Chris Airey takes us on a journey through the ups and downs of investing in digital, as a case-in-point for how we can better deal with, and get value from innovations, period. Personally, culturally, and structurally. How important it is to adapt our attitudes, first, before we tackle much else. To blend, confidently, being rational decision-makers with our own instincts, appetites, and experiences, not least of being customers ourselves. This is a fine art to master.

The "magic mix" of innovation and inertia, when we get that right enough, is what makes our enterprise durable. Too much of one or the other, and we'll be off on a tangent from the market, or travelling too slow or fast. And it's the speed and direction of each market we're in that act as our main point of reference. Markets have inertia too, which is one reason why we must fuse our outside-in experiences of being consumers, with our insiders' experiences of being enterprise leaders.

Chris is not a 'cars' guy, as we're about to find out. Yet, cars are where he, and we, start our journey together in the pages ahead. Enjoy the drive!

Chris Potts is the author of The Fruition Trilogy of business novels - Fruition, Recreation, Defriction, and the 'encore' short story, Locomotion. He is also a work and career mentor for enterprise architects worldwide.

Dedication

Authoring this book was good for my soul in terms of reflecting on what I believe about Digital and how it may help you or at least provoke a response!

Having Neil Sampson and Chris Potts on my journey was great. Thank you for making my head hurt in different ways over the years because you think differently than me. Neil reviewed and edited multiple drafts, gave tough love, and helped with the humanist perspectives. Chris, well reading his books shows some glimpses of his talent for perception and conceptual engineering.

When you read this book, please pick your own context - and interpret your analysis accordingly. Neil, during editing, (correctly) kept questioning whether this was a book about B2C or B2B, leaders or owners, organizations or companies, commercial or public good. Frankly, I got to the point of making it deliberately inconsistent because, to me, it is predominantly about situational and process data, people and technology - and how they mix well or not. I should probably rewrite this book to be more abstract... should. However, I would prefer you take it as it is and play with your internal cognitive graphics equalizer to adjust the mix to your context.

Another challenge was the word Digital - is it an adjective, adverb, noun, or just ethereal? Again, please interpret form in context. I apologize on behalf of technologists for the general abuse of language we get up to (just think Cloud for describing physical servers to make you feel good about not knowing where your data is).

Finally, this book uses theory to help understand the behaviors that allow Digital to thrive or not. Therefore, a general thank you to all those who have produced such thinking and research and who use this compounded body of work to help people be their best.

> *To my family bubble: FL, DCOA, GDD – you let me be*
> *me and I love you for that.*

Now get yourself in the right mood for this book. Imagine Digital is your cocktail, do you enjoy the taste?

Chapter One

What Good Looks Like

I'm not a "cars" guy. But if there's one thing I can appreciate, it's the unparalleled beauty of the 'pony' cars in the late 60s and even early 70s.

Steve McQueen's *Bullitt*, most notable for that awesome car chase (hugely influential on other films), cast the spotlight firmly on the '68 Mustang GT. Pure testosterone on wheels, packed into sleek lines that anyone would be proud to drive.

Even more popular nowadays, the '67 Shelby, with its gorgeous profile, is right up there with the best of them.

But for me, it has to be the '66 Mustang convertible. Pure class. You get the classic look with the open top, plenty of engine under the hood. And when you're driving one, everyone smiles at you as they know your ride is not just about utility.

That's what that classic stylish car does. Brings smiles and joy to everyone who sees it. Everyone looks. And not like looking at a Ferrari or modern supercar. People look slowly. They take it all in. They like the experience.

Styles change; only a select few stand the test of time.

Even fewer acquire the status of national—and global—heritage.

The Ford Mustang was an instant sensation when it hit the market in 1964. The concept of a four-seat high-performance sports car was wildly popular, incentivizing other manufacturers to compete vigorously in the then new market for what are termed 'pony' cars.

These compact, highly stylized coupés and convertibles heralded a classic era of American car-making that only ended with the 1973 oil crisis. This is a style that also resonated around the world with cars such as the Capri in the UK, evoking emotion.

Even then, their iconic aesthetic appeal lives on. Many automakers still pay homage to the 'pony' car's iconic aesthetic with contemporary designs. There's an active market and niche support industry for "restomod" vehicles, which restore classic models like the 1968 Ford Mustang GT Fastback with modern drivetrains, LED lights, and contemporary safety features, i.e., they put modern utility into an experience. Even now, in the early days of the attempts to convert people to EVs, iconic brand names are being used by combustion-era manufacturers to cajole the transition.

But here's what's really special…

Tom Scarpello, the CEO of Revology Cars, wanted to go further. Having worked for Ford, Jaguar, Nissan, and Infiniti, his passion for automobiles was no secret. And the 'pony' cars were his greatest passion of all.

And yet, nostalgia is a famously elusive desire. It demands a reconciliation between the past and the present, between a wistful dream and everyday realities.

Scarpello knew that classic car enthusiasts like himself wanted the *look* of the old Mustangs, but they certainly didn't want to sacrifice all the comforts and conveniences of modern cars.

He wanted to admire the curves of a vehicle that would fit in perfectly in a period film or a display in an automotive museum— until he got behind the wheel, turned on the engine, and stepped on the accelerator.

Restomod cars could only go so far. He wanted a vehicle built from scratch, with all-new materials and the best that 21st-century engineering and manufacturing had to offer.

Under his leadership, Revology received Ford certification, which allowed it to make and customize cars officially under the Mustang brand. They manufacture 100% new steel car bodies that reproduce the classic silhouette of Mustangs made between 1965 and 1969.

Revology cars are holistically engineered to match contemporary standards of safety, fuel economy, emissions, drivability, and comfort. Once you get behind the wheel, there's no mistaking the fact that its impressive performance and luxurious interior depend on technologies that simply didn't exist in the 60s.

However, Revology has a constant challenge to confront. No matter what type of car they work on, they must always work to a set of constraints. Revology's engineers must work within the limitations and specifications of the classic Mustang shells that they reproduce.

For example, they only have so much engine space available to them. This means they have to make tough decisions about the types of engines they use. Having the best of both worlds sounds great in theory, but this is difficult to achieve in practice. Revology's customer base ultimately expects a very specific aesthetic from their vehicles. Meanwhile, Revology must also ensure that all its vehicles comply with the Federal Motor Vehicle Safety Standards (FMVSS). For example, Revology can't install airbags in a Mustang without adjusting its appearance.

So, what's a classic car reproduction and re-engineering organization to do?

You can think of Tom as the one who brings everything together into a cohesive whole.

For example, let's say that a customer comes in who wants a specific body shape. So far, so good. However, that customer will usually have some bespoke requests as well. Perhaps they want a particular set of wheels or want the vehicle to incorporate a modern suspension system that may not be suitable for it.

Retromod or Digital, there's always trade-offs.

Hopefully, you have not been skimming too fast and noticed that this book started with a non-digital example quite deliberately. It is one of my beliefs that many people seem to take a different approach to Digital than other organizational decisions. Interestingly, I find that when some organization leaders treat digital projects like a make/buy decision, for example, such as refurbishing the lavatories, technologists can struggle to accept the debate or rationally explain their point of view. Another example is that frequently, there are assertions that a company should start again on a platform, which is odd given that software code cannot wear out like machinery for fabric. I accept that digital has some differences in the expanded range of possibilities and reduced constraints. However, some elements, such as the ability to add art and flair to essential software engineering, have many parallels to other skills. Outcomes that are more than the sum of the parts are the essence of the theme of this book.

There are many reasons that software and data platforms fail at some point. Digital leaders must be able to explain how investments will be well-considered and sustainable. Would you accept anything less in any other personal or business investment?

In a digital project scenario, you can think of the customer as a digital project stakeholder. They'll have all sorts of things that they want their project to do. The developers then compare that list of requirements to what's actually possible and work with the stakeholders to arrive at a solution.

The same thing happens with Revology and their cars. Tom gathers the desired specs from the customer and then he turns to his team. If there's a specific suspension request, he has an expert in suspension systems tell him if the request is even possible. If the customer wants to install a particular set of wheels or wants a specific type of upholstery, Tom has experts he can consult with to determine if the request is even viable. Simply put, he has this incredible team of experts who can tell him how to trade off what's possible and what isn't.

The key is that these experts need guidance. They need somebody at the helm who can gather all the data, communicate with every key stakeholder, agree on priorities, and mix all the ingredients together to come up with something viable and keep the customer happy.

That's Tom—our mixologist. I know you were probably expecting a cocktail mixologist; that will come. What is life without a little tease?

In the case of Revology, the mixologist is there to bring all the pieces together. They're the one person in the organization who really knows what they're talking about and is capable of gathering the data to come up with a solution. By data, I mean listening to elicit the whole range of what is termed left or right brain customer requirements, as well as technical specifications.

Most importantly, the mixologist can then coordinate a team of experts within the organization to deliver a product that best fits the customer's requirements while working within the restraints that apply to the project. Critically, the mixologist has to be able to make the best possible choices without embarking on the classic, and often costly, approach of building everything from scratch.

And that idea of building or buying from scratch (as per the old days of software packages and the evolution to SaaS and PaaS) brings me to one of the main concepts I'll talk about in this book— the digital mixologist.

In much the same way that Tom has to find a way to work within physical constraints, you, as the leader of a digital endeavor, must find a way to work within the limitations that the available technology places on you and the constraints an organization will test you with.

As the digital leader, you must not embark on the classical IT mission of rebuilding everything from scratch or to the latest fashion before anyone gets an ounce of new value. Instead, you must be or find a mixologist capable of collecting data, understanding the restrictions, bringing knowledge or experience, adding flair and stretch, and thereby mixing all of the ingredients into a digital cocktail that satisfies your customer's needs timely and affordably.

And there's a critical component of this that I haven't touched on yet—your organization's culture.

Tom would fail in his role as a mixologist if the culture around him didn't play to the same high standards and collaborative ethos that he sets. The key to culture is that your people treat the customer with the same high standards that they would expect themselves if they were the customer. This is easier said than done when you are supply-side as you understand all the problems and challenges whilst a customer shouldn't generally have to care.

> *As the mixologist, you can experiment to be more playful and disruptive to fuse the situational legacy with the art of the possible.*

In doing so, you create both a personalized customer experience and a culture that encourages your people to adapt to the changes around them and resist the pervasive commoditization of aspiration. It can be depressing in the realm of digital, where, in theory, the possibilities are endless that we look to the same old software packages and SaaS platforms and become creatively numb under the indoctrination of their training and the allure of commercial and reputational safety.

It is in the adaptation of vision to reality that many cultures struggle. We often see culture as this static thing that doesn't need to change, that we must all absorb to our bones, that has got us to where we are now. The result is the virus of inertia, as an organization relies on what apparently worked before despite all of the modern advancements around them imploring them to change. If we come back to the Revology story, we see an example of an organization adapting old cars to suit its clientele's modern demands. Without those adaptations, the vehicles would be of little use to anybody outside of classic car collectors. They would remain products of their time, superseded by the modern cars of today. They have dispassionately analyzed the past and chosen to retain the winning facets such as style and fun.

This is the effect that digital change can have on your organization. The rapid pace of change in the digital sphere can potentially leave your organization and its culture in the dust. While you focus on what used to work, others adapt. They take risks, skip technology phases, and plot how to get an edge. They have a sophisticated view of risk. They enhance their organizations for the future so that they're able to provide their customers with what they need as well as become more attractive to potential customers and markets. And in doing so, they're able to create a positive difference, even as the pervasive effects of digital and data become more pronounced, they create adaptive momentum.

My message in all of this is a simple one:

Your organization needs to adapt if you want digital that is useful, usable, and used, as well as a culture that is open to ongoing innovation from technology.

And ultimately, this adaptation to discerning mixology is a people aptitude and attitude challenge, which brings us right back to culture and how your organization operates. The ideas and approaches that got you through all of the risks and ways of working in the past aren't going to work for the deep, data-laden future that you now face. You may see the technology hype cycles passing by, but do you see the fundamentals and have a strategy?

Good news; you don't need to fear this change. Enjoy the ride, play with ideas, experiment, and apply a little nous. In overcoming your resistance to change—your inertia—you have the potential to improve what you have today and make it suitable and sustainable for the future.

Be like the cars that Revology builds and adapt to the needs of the modern consumer, while retaining your classic appeal.

Be like Tom Scarpello, or find somebody like him, who can act as the digital mixologist who enables you to bring everything together.

Now, in talking about culture, I'm reminded of the approaches that organization owners typically consciously or unconsciously take to serving their customers:

- The Outside-In Approach
- The Inside-Out Approach.

Only one of these approaches will work in the digital age, so it's worth examining each.

The Outside-In Approach

The qualitative and quantitative needs,
not the digital thing (aka product).

This is the core philosophy of the outside-in approach. In this approach, an organization's people become completely immersed in the way their customers think. Instead of looking for ways to satisfy existing demand, they look for ways to expand upon it within the bounds of reachable competences. Building from knowledge gathered at the ground level, they identify needs that even their customers haven't necessarily identified for themselves. In other words, you look at your organization and, ultimately, your products, from the perspective of your future customers. This enables you to develop solutions that change the paradigm for entire markets.

In his interview with Harvard Organization School, leadership expert Ranjay Gulati points to the American technology retail chain Best Buy as an excellent example of an organization he believes has an outside-in philosophy.

As retailers like Walmart branched out into technology, Best Buy recognized that it had increased price competition. Coupled with the expansion of online retailers, Amazon being the most prominent, the organization realized that it needed to make some changes. It began with segmenting its customer base, revealing that 55% of the organization's customers were women. However, this market segment tended not to enjoy shopping in Best Buy because the stores were developed by men and geared predominantly towards men. Its stores weren't laid out in a way that conformed to women's buying behavior, and even its support staff weren't always trained in how to provide their services in the specific ways that women wanted them.

So, we see Best Buy identify a reality in the market that suggests that female shoppers make up most of its customer base. It also recognizes that the ethos behind its store design isn't geared toward this specific demographic. As a result, though it's perhaps offering the products that this segment of customers wants, it's not providing them with the experience they need when they enter a Best Buy store. This realization led to the organization completely re-engineering its stores.

This is far from the only example of an organization with an exemplary customer-centric approach.

In 2015, Steve Easterbrook took over as the CEO of McDonald's. Despite still being one of, if not *the*, most dominant names in fast food, the organization faced ever-intensifying pressure from competitors, such as Taco Bell. The evolving tastes of the market compounded the challenge, leading to the organization needing to adapt its product offering to maintain its position as the "top dog" in fast food.

Easterbrook implemented a new feedback-gathering campaign in which McDonald's gathered customer insight from a range of sources, including online surveys and social media. Parsing through the data helped the organization understand what its customers wanted, thus allowing it to identify opportunities. Easterbrook's work led to introducing the "All Day Breakfast" in a range of McDonald's US stores. This approach has also led to the introduction of automated "easy order" kiosks in McDonald's restaurants, in addition to a delivery partnership with Uber Eats. These innovations are still spawning innovation in apps and segmented promotions via social media.

Again, it's all about listening to customers and giving them what they want. Or, perhaps more accurately, it's about figuring out how your customer defines and values quality as it relates to your product or service and then ensuring you provide that level of quality. We'll dig into this concept later in the book when we examine the concept of "quality of ambition."

McDonald's is also not the only organization leveraging insights from social media data to determine direction. The beauty and makeup brand Glossier has been doing this for its entire existence.

Founded by the author of the blog *Into the Gloss*, Emily Weiss, Glossier was built on the backs of the community that Weiss developed through her writing. She was plugged into what her audience wanted from the get-go as she interacted directly with that audience via her blog. When it came time to launch her organization, Weiss focused on maintaining and building the community she'd already created around her brand.

This community continues to play a key role in determining what products Glossier offers. Emily runs regular Q&As on social media, alongside using other feedback mechanisms, to find out what her community thinks about her ideas and what they want to see from Glossier.

Again, the information comes from outside the organization. And it's used to directly influence the direction that Glossier takes.

We see a move towards prioritizing customer-centricity over product-centricity in all of these examples. This may seem obvious as to how an organization should operate. Still, the simplified mentality twist is in sourcing what your customers want rather than promoting what you have bought or built.

You can see the same thing in the overview of Revology that I provided earlier. It would be easy for the organization to create customized Mustangs based on their beliefs and offer them to the market. However, the organization consults with its customers, discovers what they need, and then works to create a vehicle that comes as close to fulfilling those needs as possible within the constraints applied to them.

Reaching this level of customer-centricity requires an organization to go on a journey.

The Four Levels of Outside-In

During the same interview with Harvard Organization School, Ranja Gulati outlined what he believes are the four levels of the outside-in approach to organization. Each level is a stage of evolution in how an organization approaches what it does. Not all companies will reach, or even need to reach, the fourth level. But in your mission to adapt to the encroaching demands that digital places on your organization, you must understand the levels to plan to move through them logically and seamlessly.

Gulati's levels are as follows:

Level 1

At this level, companies take a complete product focus, which I'll discuss in more depth when discussing the inside-out approach. The organization believes that if they build something, the customer will buy it, or marketing can overcome poor fit for the customer. The focus lies more in achieving technical excellence than creating something specific to the customer's needs.

Level 2

At this level, the organization begins developing a deeper understanding of its customers. Typically, it will conduct market research and may even carry out some segmentation studies. This allows for greater targeting to be applied to product development.

However, many companies struggle to move beyond this level. They enter into a complacent mindset in which they believe their research gives them a perfect understanding of the market and what it wants. The organization still has a product-centric approach, though its research begins to permeate its sales methods. The key challenge is that this research doesn't permeate other organization areas, specifically product development. The organization still creates products independently of the research. As such, it uses its research to focus more on who to target with its products rather than on how to create products to suit the market's needs.

Level 3

Here, we begin to see a larger shift in both actions and the mindset behind the organization. The focus moves from developing products to solving the customer's challenges. As a result, the organization creates a deeper understanding of its customers' deep-rooted issues and adapts to address the problems. We see this perfectly in the example of Best Buy, which identified a customer segment with specific needs that its stores didn't fulfill. Upon identifying the needs, Best Buy adapted its stores to provide solutions. At this level, the organization tends to start building bridges between its various silos, thereby allowing the customer-centric approach to begin permeating through all levels of the organization.

Level 4

Gulati defines this level better than I ever could when he says:

> *"At level 4, firms become agnostic about whether they produce all the inputs they provide to their customers and, akin to a general contractor in construction, look for ways to assemble the appropriate pieces that may go into tackling customers' challenges."*

Sounds a bit like mixing, no?

Think back to what Revology does for its customers and you see a perfect example of this approach in action. The organization isn't as attached to its products as it is to ensuring the product tackles the specific issues and needs that the customer places in front of them. In Revology's case, this means finding ways to implement specific modern technologies into classic cars, and it will call upon a network of experts and partners to find out what's possible. Therefore, the organization is less concerned about using its own products and ideas to solve the customer's problem and more concerned with the simple act of solving it!

Outside-In vs. Inside-Out

So, we have established that the outside-in approach focuses on the customer and their needs. But what is the inside-out approach?

I've already touched on the answer by highlighting some contrasts between customer- and product-centric approaches. An organization that operates on inside-out thinking places its focus on the internal. Its primary concern is the product and the tools, processes, and systems required to make that product a reality and put it out into the market. With this approach, the customer's needs and perspective have little, if any, effect on making the product. Decisions are made based on what you think is best for the organization or customers.

Or, to put it as simply as possible…

You think you know what's best for your customers because you know all the true complexities and hardships of doing the work in your organization. As a result, you have little interest in learning about their needs or figuring out their perspective because they don't fully understand your situational experience.

You believe that you don't need to ask any questions because you already know all of the truths.

This is the real danger of the inside-out approach. If you genuinely believe you have all the answers, how do you respond when things don't go your way? How can you change what you've built if you believe you have to be perfect or somewhat better than your rivals? How can you innovate when the customer cannot be bothered working with your organizational quirks, which come across as idiocy, dysfunctionality, or arrogant outsourcing of work under the guise of self-service?

This is how inertia forms in an organization's culture. This idea that "you know best" means that you fail to adapt to what the markets could tell if only you would ask and listen. And the ultimate result is that you get left behind. At best, you engage in guesswork or initiatives, hoping to land on a product or service that your customers may want.

This approach is much like the party game "Pin the Tail on the Donkey." In the game, you have a picture of a donkey hung up on a wall and a tail, with a pin, in your hand. You're blindfolded and your task is to try to pin the tail as close to the donkey's rump as you can. The person who gets the closest is the winner.

It's a game of almost pure guesswork. Sure, you may have a feeling for the general direction you need to go in, as you can see from the donkey before the blindfold is applied. But when it's time to make your way to the donkey and pin your tail, you're blind and thus can't see what you need to see to make the right choice. Inside-out thinking blinds you in much the same way. In failing to understand the customer's needs and perspective, you're relegated to taking shots in the dark, hoping you might get lucky and hit the target. Sometimes, that happens. But in the vast majority of cases, you end up stumbling around in the dark while the person who lifts the blindfold delivers what the customer needs. The donkey can also inconveniently walk off!

Sadly, the cultural problem is even present in many parts of the digital ecosystem, such as start-ups, where it even has a special name for the "product/market fit" phase (ironically). Indeed, there is a whole range of ideologies in the start-up world where they are taught that this is an apparently efficient way to be successful. Since inside-out seems a natural human bias, we should be ever more suspicious of it.

To summarize, we can highlight the following key differences between the inside-out and the outside-in approaches:

- Outside-in focuses on improving the customer experience ahead of changing or designing products. If you're not serving a real or latent future customer need, serious questions are asked about the relevancy of the product or feature.

- Following this, the outside-in approach aims to maximize the benefits delivered to the customer. By contrast, even the best inside-out organization will just seek to validate its point of view. In both cases, we see an emphasis on improving internal inefficiencies and overcoming now unhelpful accumulated experience or methods. The critical difference is that the outside-in approach focuses on doing this to enable the organization to better address the pain points it discovers in its customers.

- In the outside-in approach, all processes, policies, and systems are built around what you learn from your customers. With inside-out, these are all developed separately from any interaction you may have with customers. Again, you know best.

This idea of "you know best" is the crucial cause of the inertia that so many organization leaders experience, especially in current times when the shift to digital is accelerating. You vainly struggle to adapt to your customers' needs because doing so means that you have to accept the fact that you don't have all of the answers. Ego or fear of risk gets in the way of service, and your inability to even ask profound questions, never mind adapt to the answers, leads to a state of inertia.

The paper *Investigating Strategic Inertia Using* OrgSwarm (A. Brabazon, A. Silva, T.F. de Sousa, M. O'Neill, R. Matthews, E. Costa) identifies two fundamental forces that feed into this inertia:

- Imprinting Forces
- Market-Selection Forces.

Both forces feed into this idea that the organization owner has all of the answers already, with the result being that they struggle to adapt. In the case of imprinting forces, we see how the initial decisions made in setting up the organization impact it later. Those initial decisions feed into every decision made in the future, leading to them becoming ever more profoundly imprinted into the organization in the process. This imprinting creates a sense of inertia, particularly regarding organizational structure. We even see this imprinting in the relationships formed with vendors and suppliers. This enormous web of imprints works right up until the point where the industry, or the customers' needs, evolve. And the challenge lies in undoing all of these imprints to create a more useful strategy.

Similarly, we have market-selection forces that seem to push us towards creating stability. After all, the companies that consistently achieve this stability are more likely to establish themselves in the marketplace. As such, the most efficient organizations often tend to display structural inertia, if for no other reason than the need to enable greater complexity as the organization grows. As a result, the organization struggles to adapt simply because stability and a sense of inertia are built into it for it to succeed in the market. Of course, once the market changes, that stability becomes the organization's "ball and chains," as the complex structures it created simply can't comprehend nor subsequently provide what the customer needs on a timely basis.

Ultimately, it all comes down to having the ability to ask good questions and, crucially, adapt based on the answers.

And this brings me to another concept that you must understand as you seek to make digital effective.

You Don't Have the Silver Bullet (That's Okay!)

In mythology, a silver bullet is the only way to slay a werewolf. Thus, the concept of the "silver bullet" means to find the single solution that solves a given problem. In this case, the bullet solves the issue of the werewolf rampaging through the streets and leaving a trail of destruction in its wake. In the organization world, the "silver bullet" is often a term applied to the search for a solution or technology that can solve every problem that you have. Perhaps it is just a mindset of hope for leaders who don't have the right data or backing.

This idea of a silver bullet creates yet another set of challenges that prevent an organization from adopting the outside-in philosophy.

Firstly, the belief in the existence of a silver bullet limits the range of questions that you ask. For example, if you believe that a specific technology provides the perfect solution to an internal problem, you set your expectations for the answer. You think nothing else needs to be considered, so you stop asking questions. As a result, if the solution fails to deliver everything you expected, the focus falls on how you must have incorrectly implemented it rather than whether more consideration needs to go into developing a solution.

Secondly, the idea of a silver bullet existing means that you believe there is a single answer to whatever problem you face. And frankly, this is never the case in an organization. Every challenge that you confront, from developing internal processes through to delivering what your customers need, has multiple solutions. In chasing the silver bullet, you limit yourself to a single answer while ignoring all other possible solutions. For example, an organization that fully believes its product is a silver bullet is unable to see that it may not meet the needs of the customer. This leads to them continuing to push the product even as the market tells them it's not what they want. Additionally, these organizations are not stupid in that they often market to executives creating a personal risk downside for playing with something else that could deliver more benefits.

My message here is simple…

> *There is no such thing as a Digital silver bullet either.*

There is no single correct approach to any of the challenges that you face now or in the future. And it's in chasing the silver bullet strategy that you limit your approach, create inertia, and ultimately develop a culture that can't adapt to customers' needs. You don't have the silver bullet. You can't have the silver bullet. If you did, by some miracle, have one, you probably wouldn't know without the correct data analytics to back it up that you aren't just shooting the donkey. Additionally, what you think is a silver bullet is probably a transitory relief as the werewolf species mutates and evolves.

And that's okay!

Pursuing the silver bullet comes down to this need to believe that you have all the answers and the world is or should be fully controllable and not organic. It's this belief that fuels the inside-out approach, and it's this belief that leads to organizations struggling to adapt to the market. And it's this belief that stops you from asking questions. It's a naive belief that the world is not an ever-changing, messy problem. You have such a deep-seated conviction that you have the answer you're incapable of asking questions, as the answers you receive may reveal that you're wrong, which we are all conditioned to avoid.

This is a critical barrier that you must overcome to develop a customer-centric organization.

The C-suite must consider a reality without silver bullets. Digital leaders must not hear C-suite questions on investment, service, or outcomes as an insult to their silver bullet solution on which they have hung their self-esteem.

However, it's not the only barrier. Beyond the steadfast belief that only you have the answer to any challenge your organization faces, you have the obstacle of believing that you know what your customers need better than they do. In your mind, you're trying to help the customer by providing them with a solution to a problem they might not even know exists. And this extends to how you treat your people and the culture you develop. Through your desire to be the person with all the answers, you become a leader who never allows your people to experiment for themselves. Everybody follows your way of doing things ("the right way"), which means they never figure out things for themselves. As such, they never stretch or grow, which feeds into a culture of stagnation over innovation. In essence, we see the shadow of the leader looming large over the entire organization and suffocating it. Your behavior and attitude shape the culture you create, and your people ultimately adopt these behaviors and attitudes. Often, leaders do this unconsciously. In trying to enforce their way of doing things, they influence the actions of those inside the organization using their guile, super skills, and positional power. The organization's people absorb said leader's values, mirroring their behavior while living under the shadow of the leader. The Leadership Shadow was first published in 2014 by Champions of Change in collaboration with Chief Executive Women and based on an adaptation of a model provided by Pine Street, the leadership development group of Goldman Sachs.

Think of your leadership shadow as a reflection of everything that you say and do within your organization. This shadow affects your people, whether you realize it or not. It is your job to ensure the shadow you cast is a positive one that delivers the right cues to your team.

In other words, it's up to you to cast a shadow that doesn't cause your people to believe that the only correct way to do things is your way.

It's also true to say that culture is made up of many leaders' shadows in established organizations that can form into myths and legends that are hard to change. Therefore, it is vital that all leaders working in digital are conscious of the shadow cast on the team to ensure that they use their human potential and don't quietly quit.

All of this leads to the third barrier that chasing the silver bullet creates—your need for control and your/organizational fear of never being wrong.

In being the person who "provides the answer," you maintain control and acclaim. You're the person who drives the conversation forward and dictates its terms. And you believe that's how it should be as you're the leader of the organization. Only you truly understand the customer. But again, this need for control prevents your people from growing. They become less empowered and less curious to seek data insight because they're always following your lead instead of being able to contribute their ideas and answers.

Again, we can refer to Revology to see the opposite of this in effect. Tom Scarpello never assumes he has all the answers when a customer requests some bespoke addition to a car. He doesn't try to give them a silver bullet right away. Rather, Tom goes back and talks to his experts. He encourages the people on the ground to see if what the customer wants fits into the mix of constraints and previous trade-offs. And if Revology can't provide exactly what the customer wants, more questions get asked until it reaches a solution that's viable and good for the customer's desired outcome. No doubt, the Revology team gets to know many common requests and solutions over time but has learned to deliver that knowledge in a way that gives the mixology customer experience.

The desire to find a silver bullet, and even the inherent belief that one exists, can affect decision-making at every level of your organization. It can lead to the creation of biases, which again feed into inertia.

The Danger of Your Biases

Your cognitive biases are both a danger and a defense mechanism. On the one hand, these biases act as a sort of mental shortcut, allowing you to use what you've learned and experienced in the past to fast-track decision-making. That's particularly important in a world where we're bombarded with information. Instead of struggling with the impossible task of comprehending everything you're presented with, your cognitive biases allow you to take a shortcut to what will hopefully be a good decision. As a defense mechanism or survival instinct, this works wonderfully.

As an innovative force?

Not so much.

Our biases affect our thinking to such a degree that they can make us prone to errors of judgment. They can lead us to think that what we've experienced in the past and the biases we've built due to those experiences mean that we already have all of the answers.

But, in reality, our biases often get in the way of genuinely innovative thought. They can restrict creativity, stifle imagination, and prevent us from seeing when what worked before is no longer suitable for the current environment, particularly when we don't allow space for researching, examining data, or thinking.

It's all about keeping us on the "safe" path. In their Nobel Prize-winning research, Amos Tversky and Daniel Kahneman spoke about a phenomenon called "anchoring." This term refers to how biases held by decision-makers lead to irrational choices that affect global economies. In the organization space, we can look to anchoring as something that pushes us towards the tangible and the structural. When the mind attempts to wander in more creative directions, it's the anchor that holds it back and prevents it from fully exploring the options. And so, the decisions we make invariably come back to that anchor because we "know" that sticking with what we've learned is a safe thing to do.

The Curse of Knowledge

Our cognitive biases are a curse and Achilles' heal of knowledge. They push us into a situation where we rely on our past experiences and what we've learned or mislearned from them to make decisions. You believe you know better only because something proved you right in the past. And any previous success you've experienced while applying this knowledge reinforces the belief that you're on the right path. And again, this will work fine when everything's going well for your organization. But as soon as the paradigm shifts and market forces begin demanding something different, you're left stuck. You're so lost in this prison of belief in the way things were, you find it much harder to imagine alternatives and innovate. Your personal defense mechanisms create more inertia. This can be particularly problematic when the market environment changes rapidly for PESTLE reasons and/or profoundly as per pandemics or ESG emergence.

These mentions of PESTLE and ESG lead us to the obvious question of what both of these things are.

PESTLE is an acronym that stands for Political, Economic, Sociological, Technological, Legal, and Environmental. When we discuss PESTLE, we're examining the impact that any of these six areas can have on the decisions we make in our organizations. For example, a regulatory change requiring you to alter how you manufacture your products creates a PESTLE-based change in your market environment. You have new legal restrictions to work within, challenging what you previously knew about your market. Of course, the technological example is one of the easiest of the six to grasp. As new and disruptive technologies emerge, your organization needs to adapt by incorporating said technologies into your systems and processes. Failure to do so by sticking to what you know instead of what the market tells you will lead to inertia as your competitors overtake you.

ESG stands for Environmental, Social, and Governance. It's a term commonly used by investors to denote companies that are highly environmentally or socially responsible or operate in the realm of risk management. It is also often used by roles within corporate governance to workstream the impact the organization has on the world. ESG becomes a key issue if you hope to attract investment from those who value these particular qualities. And as we see with PESTLE, the malleability of environmental and social issues can impact what you know about your market and its desires. For example, many investors, alongside a large number of customers, will feel wary about giving any money to an organization that is not environmentally responsible in the modern age. If you do nothing to lower your carbon footprint, you end up stuck in an old way of operating the organization that others have long since surpassed. Again, we see inertia in play as internal resistance to these types of changes is common.

Whether you see this interia being right or wrong in terms of the ESG/carbon footprint we should leave to one side; the point here is related to your response to outside-in demand and the curse of knowledge of present economics vs future outcomes.

You will likely see this inertia in action whenever you attempt to implement change in your organization, especially from those who've worked as part of your team for a long time. These settled team members have this curse of knowledge as they've seen the previous approaches' successes or failures, whether or not they really learned the right lessons from those experiences. As such, they're incredibly resistant and frequently passive-aggressive towards ideas that may require them to diverge away from what they've always known. Even though they're not always consciously aware of the fact, their decision-making relies on the shortcuts they've developed through experience. Unfortunately, that same experience becomes an anchor at another time when customers' needs evolve.

Breaking this type of thinking requires practice on your part. It requires you to identify the existence of your anchor, your biases, and the latent constraints of collective accumulated biases or groupthink in the first place. It also requires you to rally against them actively when they appear in your decision-making. Without practice, you fail to keep your biases in check. In turn, those biases affect every aspect of your decision-making. In practice, this often leads to you focusing on the wrong problems, confusing cause with effect, symptoms with ailments, etc., as seen in the inside-out model. Instead of trying to solve a customer's problem, you naturally make decisions based on your internal processes and beliefs, regardless of the end product that the customer receives. Worse yet, your biases may mask critical flaws in your plans, leading you to repeat the same patterns you've always repeated.

You Must Ask Questions

There is another critical component in how our biases form. Experience teaches us that a particular approach works, which means we may apply it long after it's outdated and the market has moved on. However, your biases also strengthen when they go unchallenged. When you have nobody to point out that your decision may not be the best solution for your customer, you essentially receive approval for that decision. This feeds into the belief that you know best, making it harder to escape your biases the next time you need to make a decision.

How do you escape this cycle?

You must ask questions as a means of listening! You must take time to reflect and devise outcomes from the noise.

The key to this is to listen to understand rather than listen as a means of waiting for your opportunity to reply. Pay full attention when somebody is talking to you; demonstrate the skill of active listening. This means taking note of their body language and what is happening with their eyes just as much as you listen to the words they're saying. Avoid interrupting and show that you're engaged through physical actions, such as leaning in and making eye contact. Instead of jumping straight into a response, try repeating or summarizing what the other person says, thus demonstrating your understanding. In doing this, you listen to understand, which enables you to offer more considered and thought-provoking responses. This, in turn, makes the questions you ask more valuable because you understand the answers you're given.

And this brings us back to comparing the inside-out and outside-in philosophies. By its very nature, the inside-out approach prevents you from asking the right questions or challenging confirmation bias. Customers, and perhaps even internal stakeholders, get excluded from the decision-making process. Their opinions aren't necessary as you're the leader, and you know what they need better than they do. As a result, you don't hear the dissenting voices, the varying opinions, or even any customers' miscomprehension that could help you understand the route you should take. By contrast, the outside-in approach invites opinion. It invites criticism and enables you to question your ideas based on what you learn from customers and those within your organization from their rational or equally valid emotional perspectives. Ultimately, through outside-in, you overcome your biases and begin making decisions that are vital to a sustainable organization. Customers who are not listened to always have social media to share their views with other potential customers!

Your organization's strength comes from the ability to ask the right questions and adapt to the market's needs. You're really not displaying "weakness" when you admit you don't have all the answers. Instead, you demonstrate a desire to learn more, to understand what your customers need and how you can best provide for them.

All of this isn't to say that your past experiences are worthless. It's not to say that what you've learned in the past has not proven to be the direction that you best take in the future. Instead, I aim to inform you that those lessons can become outdated. The thinking behind them may come from another time and said thinking won't necessarily lead to wise decisions as your market evolves. Dispassionate analysis and synthesis may provide ingredients for the digital mix but solutions must be appropriate for the serving.

Perhaps the key lesson here is that time stands still for no one. So why should your digital be electronic concrete?

I'm reminded of the old story of King Canute as I write this. Yes, you are getting a fable in a digital business book. The legend goes that England was once ruled by a man named Canute, who was believed to be the wisest and most powerful man of all. Everywhere he went, his followers would bombard him with flattery, telling him he was the greatest man ever. Here, we have situations that could easily lead to cognitive bias forming. After all, if a great number of people tell you that you're the greatest, you're sure to believe them, right?

Canute recognized the danger of this way of thinking. So, one day, he questioned his subjects. He commanded them to bring his chair to the beach and place it on the edge of the water. Sitting down, he said, "I notice the tide is coming in. Do you think it will stop if I give the command?"

Baffled at first, his followers soon decided to affirm what they'd always said. Canute was the most powerful man in existence, so, of course, the tide would retreat at his command. After all, everything else that he commanded had happened in the past. Upon hearing this, Canute ordered the tide to retreat, telling the water that it dare not touch his feet. Of course, the tide kept coming in and eventually, the water lapped around his ankles. And at that moment, Canute shattered the biases that surrounded him.

In this story, Canute confronts the biased beliefs that his followers have about him as he was sufficiently wise and self-aware. He shows those biases for what they are—risky, lazy assumptions based on past information that does not consider a change in circumstances. In the organizational world, the inside-out approach leads to us making these types of biased decisions all the time. We often operate based on hunches rather than on what we learn from our customers. As a result, we engage in strategies with unknown amounts of opportunity cost or unintended consequences. Of course, when these strategies fail, we begin talking about the need to "pivot," creating vacuums of inefficiency and confusion in the process. Clear strategy failure is actually a better outcome than the more usual "meh" results.

We're always trying to pin the tail on the donkey without any guidance.

Perhaps it's better to ask somebody who can see to give us a hand?

Customers are generally human and will frequently tell you what they want in emotional, process, data, and outcome terms.

The Biggest Mistake That Leaders Make

All of this leads me to what I believe is the biggest mistake that all humans, including organizational digital leaders, make:

Assuming that everybody thinks like them.

Deep down, you know that your opinion is just one of the billions that exist on the planet. And yet, you may forge ahead with decisions based on your biases in the mistaken belief that everybody else thinks as you do. And if they believe as you do, they will want the products that you develop. Or are you just a fatalist and find being so insignificant is non-processable and have to forge ahead regardless?

We can see the issues with this thinking with a simple experiment. Half-fill a glass of water and place it on a table. Then, ask as many people as possible whether they see the glass as half-full or half-empty. The fact that there is variance in the answers shows us that people see the world around them in very different ways. And if we expand this to the far more complex issues surrounding us, it's easy to see how even a small group of people will hold divergent opinions. Perhaps you think this experiment is tedious, blindingly obvious, and not worth stating, but challenge yourself. Do you actually act in a way that understands the diversity of thought and wants of your customers or the people in your organization?

But if this is the case, why is it that the people in your group (your organization) may reinforce your beliefs? For example, why is it that so many people will follow a leader down an objectively bad path without questioning the decisions that the leader is making? Perhaps here is where we see the phenomenon called "groupthink" in action. You have, of course, heard the phrase before but really what does it mean to you?

In 1971, psychologist Irving Janis introduced this term in an issue of *Psychology Today*. He'd researched the decision-making processes of groups placed under intense stress and had discovered a trend for such groups to make poor or irrational decisions. Most interestingly, the group setting should have created an environment in which such decisions were questioned. However, Janis observed that all those in the group would often follow these bad decisions, most likely due to a desire to conform or because they operated under the belief that dissent wasn't possible in the situation.

We see this in action when organizations begin to develop an "us vs. them" mentality. When things don't go their way, they double down on the decisions they've made in the past. Instead of listening to dissent or feedback from their customers, they continue to operate under the mistaken belief that they know best, even when the evidence shows them that not everybody thinks as they do. And so, we see the development of a sort of internal echo chamber. The group keeps pushing in a particular direction because of the desire to conform to the leader's choices. As such, internal dissenting voices disappear, and the group may even begin to see the customer as the enemy in the worst-case scenario. A sort of tribalism forms, which makes the group even less likely to alter its course. I consider the digital gag of "noreply" email addresses the ultimate aggressive manifestation of "us vs. customers".

Again, it's very likely that you already know much of this. You know what it is like to waste your time trying to get support from digital fortresses. You have even experienced this groupthink phenomenon before. After all, it's the same thing that King Canute rallied against when he grew tired of hearing his subjects laud him for feats he couldn't possibly have accomplished.

What you may not understand, perhaps because it seems such an old concept that applies to others and not you, is how these issues can hold you back in terms of the digital and customer experience you provide. You may guess at the data you will never get. You may not see how tribalism within your organization leads to the belief that what you do represents the visible world. And you may also struggle to see how your own biases feed into this approach and prevent you from moving towards the outside-in philosophy that enables your organization to serve its customers' needs.

To deepen your understanding of the issue, it's worth visiting some of the most prominent forms of bias and the concept of tribalism to understand what they are and how they may affect you and your impact.

Confirmation Bias

Have you ever had an inkling that a friend has an issue with you? You don't exactly know why you have this feeling, but it gnaws away at you enough that you decide to give the friend a call. You get no answer. So, you send them a text to check in with them. And again, you get no response.

The lack of answers confirms the suspicion that your friend has an issue. The result is that you end up unhappy with your friend because your friend has this unexplained problem with you. And therefore, an actual problem arises because you've developed a belief that appears to have been confirmed by the lack of response. You act as though the suspicion was correct and if left unchecked, that belief can lead to a real falling out between you and your friend, based on unpleasant passive-aggressive behavior.

This is confirmation bias in action.

Confirmation bias occurs when you believe, want, or fear a specific situation to be true. Your belief in this truth is such that you will take any "evidence" that supports it as gospel. We see this all the time when people try to prove their points through studies. Rather than objectively sifting through scientific or data rich evidence to reach an objective conclusion, they approach the search with a preconceived belief. This leads to them seeking out studies that confirm the view while consciously or otherwise ignoring any evidence that points away from it.

We form a view and then we seek evidence to confirm the theory. This, in turn, prevents us from seeking evidence that contradicts the view. In doing this, we deceive ourselves to the point where we can no longer make objective decisions.

Affinity Bias

This form of bias is all about comfort, and you can see it in action in almost any social setting.

For example, let's say you're going to a party. When you arrive, the host greets you, leaves you to explore the venue, and starts talking to people. However, you usually don't just initiate a conversation with the first person you see. Instead, you scan the rooms to find somebody you already know. Once you spot them, you make a beeline for them because being around somebody you have an affinity for gives you a sense of comfort.

This form of unconscious bias prevents you from learning about the new people at the party. You gravitate towards the person that you know at the expense of going through the uncomfortable process of meeting somebody new. Wasn't much point in the party or inviting new people that don't know anyone?

In an organization, we gravitate toward the people who seem to have an affinity for our present ideas. You've all heard of leaders who surround themselves with "yes" people. This is affinity bias in its purest form, as said leader makes it impossible to hear dissenting opinions due to the organization they keep. And perhaps that is the most significant danger of affinity bias. It causes us to seek out people who think and act in a similar way to us, in a way that we approve of. As leaders, it makes us more prone to promoting people we like over people who have the skills that a role needs. Unfortunately, affinity with the people around you doesn't always lead to good organizational decisions, especially when an organization experiences inertia. Lack of diversity therefore increases the likelihood of groupthink now and in relation to customers' future digital platforms. If there is no dissenting voices, nobody will guide you towards a new path.

Perversely, corporate governance often drives against diversity of thought or open decision-making. In his article, *Maximizing the Benefits of Board Diversity: Lessons Learned From Activist Investing*, Barington Capital Group COO Jared Landaw highlights the need for diversity and one of the reasons why this apparent drive against it may exist. He points out that the commonly held belief that introducing people from more diverse backgrounds into the boardroom will lead to higher levels of innovation is often incorrect. However, the concept of increasing diversity is not at fault here. Instead, it's often the execution of the concept.

For example, an incumbent director may set out to find a new director who comes from a different demographic than themselves. However, they are also likely to seek somebody with similar experiences, values, and knowledge. As such, the diversity gained from seeking out somebody from a different demographic is undermined by the fact that the new director shares many of the same thought patterns and experiences as the incumbent director.

And so, we see an unconscious drive against diversity of thought, even as the incumbent director makes a conscious effort to introduce diversity. By seeking somebody who they have an affinity with based on experiences and values, the incumbent director ends up failing to introduce diversity into the board.

This highlights the insidious nature of affinity bias. Even when we consciously aim to create diversity, our natural urge to seek affinity with others may lead to an unwitting push against the forms of open thought that hiring people from different backgrounds is intended to create.

Conformity Bias

In 1956, Solomon E. Asch ran an experiment that came to be known as the Asch Conformity Test. The experiment involved gathering a group of test subjects and providing them with a set of lines as follows:

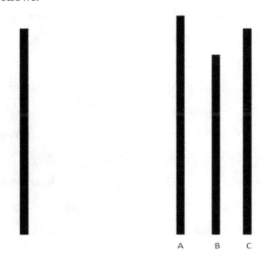

A   B   C

Participants were asked a simple question: Which of these lines, A, B, or C, matches the line on the left-hand side?

However, the test came with a twist. All but one of the "test subjects" was actually part of the experiment. Only one person was there to legitimately provide their answer. The rest were there to provide an incorrect answer that Asch asked them to give. And so, Asch asked the question of each of the participants, each of whom gave the same incorrect answer. Finally, he came to the final participant, who was the only one who hadn't been asked to give an incorrect answer.

What did he do?

He gave the same answer as everybody else, even though it was demonstrably wrong!

This is conformity bias in action. It's the overriding need to gain acceptance into a group, even when that acceptance comes at the expense of logical and correct answers. The groupthink phenomenon also often provides examples of conformity bias. People follow the crowd because they don't want to be the person who goes against the prevailing mentality. The reasons for this vary but typically come down to fear of reprisal should a person challenge or indeed dissent. It also can be driven by imposter feelings in group situations. Of course, the presence of conformity bias in your team means you're far less likely to hear opinions that differ from yours. And once again, this can result in stagnation or inertia as your organization follows the wrong path.

Conformity bias is particularly strong in digital choices around suppliers and software/SaaS. There are many good reasons to go for known quantities, but do you have the evidence to prove you are making the right situational choice? Have you measured your groupthink and bias levels lately?

Tribalism

I spoke earlier about the "us vs. them" mentality and how this can set in when you start to view your customers as "the enemy." That is tribalism in action. It's the coming together of a group of people to rally against another group.

However, tribalism often occurs within an organization as well. When you have a large group of people working for the same organization, it's natural to find each department feels it has its own goals and purpose. This is often referred to as siloing, especially when each group operates separately from the others. The issue here is that these disparate goals lead to the formation of internal tribes that damage the organization. For example, the customer care department may not be happy about the volume of complaints they're receiving and may blame the sales department. If only sales did its job right instead of promising something the organization can't deliver, the customer care department wouldn't be in this mess. Therefore, the sales department becomes the enemy, the "them," that the customer care department rails against.

This tribalism results in the breakdown of relationships in the organization and the inability to work towards a common goal. In the worst-case scenario, entire departments may refuse to work with other departments, creating an atmosphere of infighting that's never conducive to delivering a good product or service to the customer. Linking back to Outside-In this tribalism is particularly challenging for customers when they frankly don't care about your functional organization structure.

I find the most insipid element of Tribalism is the "othering" of other functions. This manifests in a lack of knowledge and data sharing that would benefit all in understanding the outside-in perspective. It seems inefficient that this integrated view is often only possible at more senior levels.

Find Your Digital Mixologist

We've covered a lot of background information in this chapter. You will now have a deeper understanding of biases and their impact on your decision-making abilities. You should also see how the inside-out approach to an organization often leaves that organization unable to listen and therefore adapt to its customers' needs.

This idea of adaptation brings me to the issue of digital and the core concept that underpins what I will elucidate in this book. In today's world, digital is the trend de jour of the long-term disruption from technologies. Any organization that fails to adapt to the ever-evolving digital landscape will become a victim of inertia and, at best, an unhappy life as a price-pressured commodity.

How do you prevent your organization from experiencing sluggishness, malaise, zombie-ness, and then morale-sapping decline?

You find somebody who has that little bit of magic to help you and your team do what you need to do. You find yourself a digital mixologist.

Who is the mixologist?

This diagram on the next page highlights some of the key traits that your digital mixologist needs to have.

Right now, you're probably an expert drinkologist rather than a mixologist. You know how it feels when a drink tastes good, but you have no idea how to mix all of the ingredients to create the drink in the first place—what are the proven elements and what are the twists. That task falls to your mixologist. Think of this person as the bartender who's able to bring everything together to create a solution that's greater than the sum of its parts.

There are so many examples of this person in our lives.

We have chefs who can pull together a host of different ingredients to create a sublime dish. We have interior designers who can bring together all sorts of ideas about color, swatches, and fabrics to create an appealing room. Ultimately, the mixologist is the person who deals with using the right ingredients to give you the outcome that a customer needs.

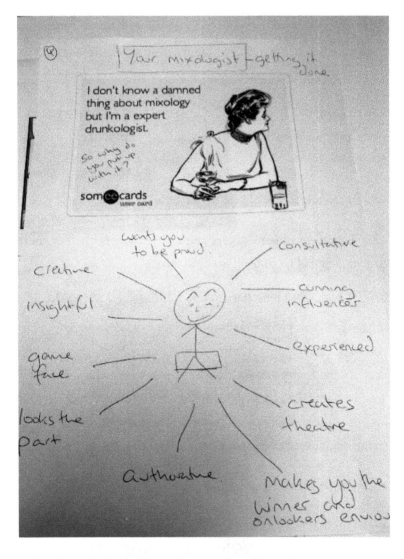

What does this look like in the digital landscape?

A digital mixologist is a person who understands what works well and can bring various technological or data ingredients together to create a whole.

They're the person who focuses on outcomes and wants to ensure the solution you provide to your customers provides them with a good experience. A digital mixologist can also provide unique insight that causes you to question how you've always done things. They're an authority in the field who can determine what you need to fuse together to create something that serves the needs of your customers.

But perhaps most importantly, a digital mixologist is somebody who pushes your organization to move away from following a method, trying to industrialize creativity, and towards delivering compelling outcomes. There may be play, trials, and experiments.

If we come to our bartender analogy, let's imagine that you tell the mixologist that you, the customer, enjoy bourbon. A good mixologist will extrapolate from that data and perhaps guide you toward a new drink that contains whisky or brandy. They'll push you to experiment with different cocktails to find something that feels right for you. As such, instead of just following the method or recipe, they'll introduce something dynamic and new for a pre-existing bourbon cocktail that may deliver a more compelling outcome.

This move from method-obsessed to outcome-focus defines a mixologist, regardless of industry.

The mixologist is the artist who can create a stunning work of art, rather than the hobbyist who paints by numbers. It's the chef who has such a deep understanding of their ingredients that they can craft unique dishes, rather than the cook who follows a recipe. In the digital realm, your mixologist is the person who can craft solutions that are unique to your customers and your organization, rather than somebody who relies on off-the-shelf products and pre-existing or vendor ideas for what "going digital" means.

Regardless of industry, all mixologists have some key traits in common. They have the confidence to experiment, which is born from understanding the ingredients available to them and the constraints that must work within. A good mixologist brings flair to the table and has a deep-seated understanding of what feels good and what makes a good product. Vitally, they are empaths looking to fuse your customer needs with organizational goals. As a digital drinkologist, you implicitly know what apps and websites you like and don't like. A mixologist can articulate the reasons for these feelings and build something from them, even when you're unable to do so yourself. They can also help your organization feed the internal rationalists through investment in ways to listen to customers and turn that into data.

By bringing a mixologist on board, you can move away from inside-out thinking and towards outside-in. The ultimate goal is to move from having this single mixologist to moving towards the organizational paradigm of mixology, in which the mixologist's qualities are reflected throughout the organization. The mixologist doesn't have a gun chamber full of silver bullets but rather has the confidence to find missing ingredients or change the cocktail with their muddling and shaking.

Doing digital is easier than it's ever been. Do you find it easy? Why? Why not?

The challenge lies in your own knowledge and constraints. It lies in your approach and the inherent biases that may inform much of your decision-making. And it lies in the ways that your people and your organization as a whole engage with the possibilities that exist.

Approaching digital investment as a risk-heavy decision is emblematic of the old way of thinking as, by implication, the thinking is inside-out. Review of any risk log and the data on opportunity risks or customer point-of-view risks are often missing. Digital is not something for you to throttle or control. It's also not something to implement based on the inside-out or delivery process methodology, or solely what a vendor or diva developer tells you. To successfully transition to digital, you need to live a little! Do some mixology and experiment with the ingredients until you find the perfect recipe. Talk to your customers, learn what they need, and focus on making your organization and people more fluid and capable of grasping opportunities. We can be far more open to ideas outside work—why so inappropriately serious about digital in work when any experience can be coded?

Test and Learn

The world keeps moving forward. People change, new trends emerge, and your competition grows ever more sophisticated. In taking the inside-out approach, you shut yourself away from these evolutions and leave yourself in a state of inertia. Only when you move to the outside-in approach can you better understand what your customers need and how you can deliver that to them on the digital level.

Bringing a mixologist onboard or becoming one yourself is just the first step. This enables you to challenge your existing organizational paradigms, help your people grow and start confronting the biases that inform your current decision-making. But to truly achieve digital transformation and build a sustainable organization, you must focus on the customer and make them truly fully profoundly present within your organization. Don't let your people be scared of your customers' needs. Delivering what your customers want is a more fulfilling way to spend your time at work.

CHAPTER TWO

The Power of Customer Confidence

So, now is the time to put your metaphor head on and role play being a customer.

Why do people go to fun places like cocktail bars?

It's an interesting question because everybody has access to the basic ingredients needed to make a cocktail for far less money at home. You can pop to the shop right now and buy bottles of wine, cans of beer, and even mixers that will last you several nights for the cost of a couple of cocktails in a bar. And yet, people still go to cocktail bars in their droves to buy what, on the surface, may appear to be overpriced drinks when compared to what you could buy or make yourself.

The reasons come largely down to confidence as well as the desire for experience.

Imagine that you're with your best friend and you decide you want to grab a couple of drinks. You wander around for a while before a chic little cocktail bar catches your eye. Immediately, you're attracted by the professional aura of this place, so you head inside and sit down on the stools in front of the bar. A few seconds later, the bar's mixologist comes up and asks what you want. Perhaps you're not really sure, so you talk for a moment about the types of drinks and flavors you typically go for. The mixologist listens to all of this, asks some questions, and turns it all over in their head. Recommendations start coming out and you follow the mixologist's guidance through a mutual instant dynamic decision tree.

The response you received to your uncertainty instills confidence within you. The confidence you are entitled to as a customer.

It is not just the conversation with the mixologist that creates this confidence. The entire environment plays a role. You know what good looks like when you enter a bar. You have that immediate feeling in your gut about whether or not this is a place where you want to spend your time. The music, décor, how the staff operates, and even the clientele all combine to create an atmosphere, nay theatre, that either feels welcoming or foreboding. The right environmental mix, coupled with the expertise of your mixologist, makes it even easier to feel confident in the quality of the customer experience that you're about to enjoy.

There's also the ease with which you can get your drinks, which plays a part in building this confidence. All you (the customer) need to do is walk into the bar, have a conversation, and order your drink. The whole thing is easy. You don't have to trudge through millions of steps or navigate a CFO or Procurement to try and get your hands on what you want. You're not like Frodo in Lord of the Rings slowly edging his way through the depths of Mordor just to accomplish a mission that you are entitled to want to be simple—like asking a human to help you. The experience is smooth, simple, easy, and entirely focused on the customer and their experience. You also did not have to invest in the extensive plethora of tools, processes, prerequisites, self-service steps, declaration of your life story, and buy the ingredients yourself just to achieve the outcome you wanted.

This, in a nutshell, is why people choose the cocktail bar above the simpler (and cheaper) act of buying booze from the local liquor shop and drinking it at home. You get to enjoy the experience, confident in the knowledge that you're getting your money's worth from the entire outing, and have a choice from a wider range than you would have invested in, even if the particular drinks themselves cost more than what you might be able to make yourself. Additionally, you are confident that your cocktail will be of OTIF (on-time in full) quality.

Why do you believe digital customer experience should be harder than an enjoyable cocktail bar?

And it is this type of fulsome, respectful experience that I encourage all organization leaders to try to create when they're serving customers. Confidence comes from the customer knowing that they are going to have a pleasurable experience. Just as you can "feel it" when you walk into a good cocktail bar, your customers can feel whether your organization is right for them in the way you speak to them, whether you place hurdles in their way, whether your people and processes hang or flow together, and just how much of an effort (friction) it is for them to access your service. I believe that people intrinsically value the quality of the time they spend with your services as well as the money value.

But here's the rub…

To create confidence in the customer, you must first have confidence in yourself and your organization. You must be like the mixologist who is so confident in their skills that they can listen to somebody talk about what they like and instantly come up with the right ideas for drinks that will suit their tastes based on their range of ingredients and expertise. You need to know what you do inside and out, allowing you to develop systems that enable access for your customers while allowing you to deliver with confidence.

My point here is that confidence is a key ingredient in the cocktail of a great organization and great digital. And in this chapter, I'm going to explain exactly why that is.

Confidence Attracts Customers

Your single friend comes up to you and starts bemoaning the fact that they can't find a partner. They're looking for some advice on how to meet people.

What do you say to them?

> *"It all comes down to confidence. People are generally attracted to those who appear secure in themselves and project a certain aura. You need to start feeling good about yourself and all of the qualities you can bring into a relationship. When you do that, you'll feel confident enough to approach somebody and strike up a conversation that might go somewhere."*

I'm not telling you anything new here. We all know that confidence plays an intrinsic part in attraction and forming new relationships. You've also likely been on the other end of the equation, speaking to someone lacking confidence. While calling this experience "off-putting" is perhaps too strong a word, their lack of confidence in themselves also makes you lack confidence in them.

But despite knowing this, so many organization leaders underestimate the crucial role that having complete confidence in themselves and the service they offer plays when it comes to the offers they make to customers. After all, good organization is about relationships. You form relationships with your organization partners, your team, your vendors, and, of course, your customers. If confidence plays such a key role in your personal relationships, it stands to reason that confidence can also help you to build stronger organizational relationships and, ultimately, attract more customers. It's the same humans, after all.

However, we also know that overconfidence can be a turnoff in our personal relationships. When somebody veers over the line that separates confidence and narcissistic arrogance, they become less appealing to us because we feel that their confidence in themselves is unjustified. Again, the same can hold true in an organization, particularly if the marketing accentuates a cognitive dissonance. If you present yourself or your service in a way that appears overly confident without justification, you will turn others off. And so, we see a delicate balance between confidence and arrogance in your relationships. The need to find this balance is emphasized in an interesting set of studies conducted by the team at the Society for Personality and Social Psychology.

The team prepared a battery of four studies designed to measure the effects of overconfidence. They explain their hypothesis as follows:

> *"We hypothesized that potential romantic targets would perceive overconfident individuals as more genuinely confident, and consequently rate them more favorably as a romantic partner."*

An interesting approach to take, given what I've just said about how overconfidence can be a turnoff in any form of relationship! The researchers measured various people's levels of overconfidence in various areas before selecting those who appeared most overconfident to take part in the tests.

The first study involved these overconfident people writing an online dating profile, which members of the target sex then read. Interestingly, this first study showed that the profiles garnered plenty of initial interest, suggesting that overconfidence can masquerade as true confidence. However, the overconfident individuals were ultimately not perceived as more attractive by those viewing the profiles, which suggests that these people had an inkling that something wasn't quite right.

Curious, the researchers then conducted a second study in which they asked the participants to examine the profiles and rate them for arrogance. The profiles created by the overconfident people were highly rated on the arrogance scale, suggesting that arrogance undercuts the positive effects of confidence in a relationship.

All of this runs counter to the initial hypothesis.

But interestingly, the third and fourth tests the researchers ran showed that overconfidence did offer some benefits. Participants were asked to imagine they were at a singles event in the third test. One of the writers of an overconfident dating profile sat at a table with somebody the participant was attracted to. They were then asked if they would approach the table and start to compete with the overconfident person for the affection of the third party.

Most said no.

The researchers then upped the ante and put some money on the line. They tasked the other study participants (not the overconfident ones) to create dating profiles of their own. They then offered them a set amount of cash to walk away from the test. However, if they chose to stack their dating profiles up against the overconfident profiles, they would earn double the amount of money if people found the new profiles more attractive.

Again, those who didn't rate as overconfident were less willing to compete for the extra money, while those who were overconfident happily competed.

And so, we see the delicate balance between confidence and overconfidence/arrogance in action. The first two studies show us that arrogance can override the benefits of confidence in terms of building relationships with others. And yet, the final two studies show us that overconfident people are more willing to compete, which may bode well for them when fighting for the affection of a partner.

The ultimate conclusion is that those who can display confidence without arrogance gain both competitive and relationship advantages. Again, I invite you to imagine that you're in a cocktail bar. Only this time, you encounter two mixologists. The first converses with you, listens to what you have to say and confidently creates a drink. The second jumps straight into making a drink that they're sure you'll like if you say that you don't know what to order. They don't listen to you while making it, but they present themselves in such a way that they appear confident in the drink they're making. Of course, your first taste of this drink shows the confidence wasn't warranted as the second mixologist delivered something that you didn't really want.

Who would you order your third drink from?

The Five Keys of True Organization Confidence

In an article for *Psychology Today,* internationally recognized performance psychology expert Dr Jim Taylor defines confidence as follows:

> *"How strongly you believe in your capabilities to learn new skills, perform at a certain level, attain a goal, or achieve your own definition of success."*

He goes on to say that confidence is the single most crucial psychological contributor to an organization's success. The lack of it makes you less able to accomplish your goals and will mean that you struggle to attract customers. And yet, we can also see that being overconfident can cause damage to your organization. Perhaps you believe that if you're not born confident, you may come across as arrogant if you try to "fake" confidence, thus leading to you failing to reap the benefits of this skill.

"Skill" is the vital word I want you to take away from that paragraph.

Contrary to what some may tell you, confidence is a skill that you can develop with the right guidance. A combination of practice and self-awareness is what ultimately leads to somebody becoming truly confident. People aren't inherently born with this skill. Instead, so many factors come into play, including the support they've received, how well they prepare and educate themselves, and their responses to both successes and failures. In the case of our mixologists, the confidence to create the right cocktail doesn't come naturally. Our mixologists must learn everything there is to know about making great drinks, which is founded on the belief that they will eventually be capable. They will likely fail many times along the way, but they will have support from an active mentor who keeps pushing them. And they will learn that the key to creating the right cocktail for a customer is to listen to what they need and tastes, fully confident in the knowledge that they can deliver on the specifications.

That is true confidence.

In the same article, Dr Taylor goes on to define the five keys to building and maintaining confidence. Each of these keys can help you build your confidence skills, though it is the combination of all five that leads to the development of true confidence needed to attract customers.

I share these five keys here with my own contributions.

Key #1—Preparation

Dr. Taylor calls preparation the foundation of confidence, and he's absolutely correct. Preparation involves everything that goes into building your organization and presenting it to your customer. It's a combination of your skills, training, experience, thoughtfulness, and resources, all of which you pour time and effort into developing.

The quality of your preparation affects how you perform when faced with a customer. The poorly prepared will always struggle to demonstrate confidence simply because they don't have faith in their abilities to solve problems and provide what the customer wants. A mixologist who's never shaken a mixer before will stumble and stutter, trying to lead the customer toward simpler drinks instead of providing what the customer wants. The prepared mixologist is the one who knows every recipe, has practiced their skills for years, and has the support needed to reinforce and build upon those skills. They have muscle memory of the processes and ingredients, so they can "walk and chew gum" at the same time by creating, delivering, and engaging simultaneously.

Key #2—Mental Skills

If preparation is the foundation of your confidence, your mental skills are what reinforce it. Dr. Taylor encourages us to think of our mental skills as a toolbox of all of the things we use to build our confidence. Such tools include positive language and aspirational thoughts, which boost our motivation. When we feel motivated by what we're doing, we're more likely to sound confident simply because we naturally demonstrate passion when we talk about the subject!

Other mental tools include your body language and how you use it to create the desired perception, the techniques you use to relieve stress, and the things you do to calm yourself when emotions run high. From this, we can gather that the confident person has the mental skills necessary to never feel panicked, regardless of the situation. They will remain as cool as a cucumber, focused on finding solutions rather than allowing challenges or anxiety to overwhelm them. And, of course, their in-depth preparation means they have faith that they will find a solution, which builds into the mental toughness they display.

We can also include the ability to recognize and overcome personal biases within these mental skills. We've already spoken about the various types of bias that can affect your decisions as a leader. The truly confident don't shy away from these biases. They're mentally strong enough to confront and recognize them for what they are. In turn, this gives them the confidence they need to overcome their biases and look at their organizations objectively.

Key #3—Adversity

It's natural for people to try and avoid adversity as much as possible. We all want to work in ideal circumstances that create the best possible environment for our success. Unfortunately, real life rarely works out that way. Everybody who succeeds in an organization has to overcome some form of adversity along the way. And if you don't believe me, you only need to spend a few minutes on the web to find that it's packed with stories of entrepreneurs who've overcome hardship to get to where they are.

The key here is that you don't see adversity solely as a set of obstacles to overcome. You should also see it as a motivator. When you overcome adversity, you reaffirm your confidence because the skills you've worked so hard to develop come to the fore. Welcome adversity and the challenges it brings into your life. Pushing past the issues that make organization tougher, be they basic problems like distractions in the office or more complex issues such as difficult assignments, will always boost your confidence.

Key #4—Support

All of the most successful entrepreneurs have support from other people. They have teams, mentors, and families who constantly bolster the confidence they have in themselves. Whenever you feel a crisis of confidence, these are the people who give you a shot in the arm. They tell you to keep your chin up and remind you of the amazing things you've already accomplished. They listen to what you are trying to say even if you are too close to the matter at heart to be fully objective.

Sometimes, the simple act of a friend telling you that they know you can do what you set your mind to is all you need to feel more confident in your abilities.

Key #5—Success

Of course, success acts as the ultimate validation of the paths we choose for ourselves. The previous four keys all build into that moment when you finally reach the goal you set for yourself. Success can come in many forms, with organizational profits being the most obvious. But success also comes from receiving compliments on your work, seeing the smiles on happy customers' faces, and even from seeing that you have a happy team.

> *Every small victory you enjoy is a success that gives a boost to your confidence.*

Unpacking Your Self-Confidence

While mastering the five keys that Dr. Taylor shares will help you to build your confidence, these keys don't account for the fact that confidence is often a fragile thing. Even the smallest of situations can affect how we feel about ourselves to the point where we struggle to exude the confidence needed to convince customers that we are the right choice for them.

Think of our good mixologist from the beginning of the chapter. After listening to the customer, the mixologist starts making the cocktail, only to slip up midway through. They drop a bottle onto the floor and receive a reprimand from the bar owner in front of the customers. In an instant, that mixologist's confidence takes a hit that can lead to them doubting their abilities. Despite having all of the skills, experience, and everything else necessary to deliver a great experience, the mixologist is now overthinking what they do, which leads to the rest of their service being delivered in an unconfident manner.

That single failure may create a perception, both in the mixologist's and the customer's mind, that the mixologist isn't fit for the job.

Now, you may read this and get the impression that I'm saying that perfection is the ultimate goal if you wish to be confident. However, this is not the case at all. As Dr. Taylor points out, facing adversity is one of the keys to developing confidence. But if we face adversity, we and others must also accept that we will fail along the way.

Perfection is not the goal, as it is simply not obtainable.

Instead, the point I wish to make here is about the impact that failures can have on our perception of ourselves and block our path. Dwelling on such minor issues can lead to us seeing ourselves as screwups. This becomes the energy that we put into our organization, with this perception of ourselves bleeding over into how others, such as our customers, see us. And so, we see that an element of "self" comes into the confidence game. I come back to one of my earlier points about how projecting confidence is as much about how we see ourselves as it is about the skills we bring to the table.

In another article for *Psychology Today,* Amy Alkon digs a little deeper into this idea of "self." The author of *Unf*ckology: A Field Guide to Living with Guts and Confidence,* Alkon presents a scenario in her article in which a new employee makes a minor technical error at work. However, this single error feeds into the view this person already has of himself as incompetent, which then feeds into his perception that others see him as a screwup. This then feeds into what the person describes as others treating him dismissively in his work.

Alkon correctly identifies that there are deeper issues than the single mistake at play here. She states that the mistake is a trigger for something far more insidious:

> *"Chances are his underlying problem, leading to his being viewed as a screwup, or at least not very good at his job, is the (non-verbal and sometimes verbal) messages he puts out about himself that reflect a lack of self-confidence."*

To convey confidence, you must first unpack yourself and the barriers that obstruct your perception of yourself as a confident person. In the article, Alkon shares three elements of "self" that allow you to both become confident and project confidence. Again, I share them here with my own thoughts.

Element #1—Self-Acceptance

I mentioned earlier that nobody is perfect and the mask we wear distorts the ability of others to value our humanity and, therefore, judge the authenticity of our contributions. Self-acceptance boils down to accepting yourself for who you are, foibles and all, so that you develop a greater understanding of both your strengths and weaknesses. The ability to accept yourself for who you are is not something that can be taught. Rather, it's a decision you make to embrace everything about you simply by virtue of accepting that these things exist. This is not saying you may not want to improve or change certain aspects; it is more about an aware realism of your starting point.

If that sounds a little "self-helpy," then I don't apologize. However, the practical aspect of accepting yourself is that it shines a lot on the aspects of you that you could stand to improve. The alternative is to "aggressively ignore," as Alkon puts it, the aspects of you that you don't want to bring to the fore. But in doing that, you fail to accept the parts of you that could use a little extra work, thereby limiting your opportunities to develop your confidence. Again, a perfect example comes from the willing decision to leave your biases unconfronted. Doing so means you never have the opportunity to develop your confidence in your ability to work without these biases. This also comes back to what Dr. Taylor discusses about facing adversity.

Without the acceptance of "self," it's impossible to confront our weaknesses and do something about them. Without knowing our weaknesses and the abstraction of our defenses to hide our weaknesses we can't be honest or adult as to our decision making within digital transformation.

Element #2—Self-Compassion

One of the dangers of driving for self-acceptance is that the act can actively damage your confidence if you focus solely on the negatives.

I can't do this, I can't do that, I must be bloody useless!

Perhaps you get lost in your perceived failings. They cloud your vision to the point where you can't see all the good you bring to the table, leading to a lack of confidence and accentuate your imposter. It's here where compassion for yourself comes into play. And honestly, this one's really simple:

Be kind to yourself.

Nobody expects you to be perfect at everything, so treating yourself as you should be will lead you on a difficult path. You're fallible. We all are. Others are and often project or transfer their issues toward or onto you. Try to see your faults as things that connect you to others, with your strengths being what you can use to build your confidence. Accept your faults for what they are and endeavor to improve, but don't be so harsh on yourself that every small failure damages your sense of "self."

A more honest acceptance of human fallibility would allow digital strategy to be seen as art.

Element #3—Healthy Self-Assertiveness

Note the use of the word "healthy" here. We saw earlier that overconfidence does nothing to help you attract other people. Self-assertiveness can lead to a projection of overconfidence if done in an unhealthy way. For example, obstinately refusing to listen to the opinions of others as you're more concerned with "winning" with your own opinion is self-assertiveness gone awry.

Healthy assertions involve(s) standing up for yourself confidently without coming off like an arse to other people. And the ability to assert yourself properly comes from the five keys we spoke about earlier, with preparation being the main one simply because it equips you with the knowledge needed to back up your assertions.

Your Customers Want the Perfect Cocktail

Now we can see that confidence is both crucial and complex as well as being subjectively measured from the perspectives of the variety of IDs and Egos that fuse to deliver a customer experience. We all know we need it. I'm not telling you anything new here. But there are nuances to confidence that are often lost on those who try to project confidence without constraints.

Perhaps we can best see confidence as a mixture of elements that combine to create an emotive or even non-functional experience for our customers. If we come back to our cocktail bar example, the experience you enjoy is a result of confidence on many levels. The confidence of the mixologist in serving your drink, the confidence of the ambiance created by the interior designer's décor, and even the confidence that other patrons demonstrate by coming to the bar all feed into the perception you develop.

When you're on the hunt for the perfect cocktail, these are the types of things that affect your thinking and, ultimately, the decisions you make. In your own organization, you must consider the facts that you need to work on to project an image of confidence to your customers. For example, people become more confident in a digital project when they receive quick answers that display technical know-how. They feel more confident when you're able to explain the project clearly and when you have users on board who buy into what you're developing. Of course, this confidence in your customers comes from how you perceive the project, your confidence in yourself and your team, and the skills that the team brings into the project.

Just as with creating a cocktail, the ingredients that go into developing a digital solution don't tend to vary. Theoretically, creating a digital solution should be a simple science, like following a recipe. But anybody who's ever had a bad cocktail knows that there's so much more to creating something spectacular than following a set of bullet points on a sheet. There's an art to delivering a product, regardless of what the product is, and confidence is one of those intangibles that play a huge role in your delivery.

Sadly, many digital projects are delivered in a context where one or more of these example issues exist:

- Someone selling an ingredient has decided what you are drinking
- No customer of the product or service has described their perfect serve
- Your team is arguing about the best bourbon and there isn't anything else in the cocktail shaker
- No one has made many cocktails before, so they are reading a manual behind the bar on opening night
- There are a bunch of forms to fill in before getting to the bar and you can't prove where you lived five years ago
- The cocktail is sitting on a bar top in a room with no tables, chairs, or music
- If the first drink isn't liked, then all the bar staff are fired

- Drink consultants prevent the mixologist from talking to the customer and their fees are added to the bill
- Management has decided you have to sell only drinks that other bars sell
- There is no record of your visit or whether you were happy, so the next time you visit will be the same.

Perhaps I can sum all of this up succinctly:

If you're not confident in your ability to deliver a defined valued experience, you won't attract customers because they won't feel confident in you! Take this thought a bit further and you can understand that since your organization is made up of people, if you don't feel collectively confident, then the whole solution you put in front of customers will not feel right. Digital can make this issue worse without the dynamics of human interaction to read between the lines. It can make a poor experience colder. Take some time to think what you are not confident about in your organization and how digital could accentuate that lack of confidence and create enduring perceptions in customers.

CHAPTER THREE

Delivering Digital and Creating Productive Change in Your Organization

A t the conclusion of the previous chapter, I mentioned that creating the perfect cocktail might feel like it should be as simple as following a recipe. What stops you from doing it all if you have all the ingredients? You may feel the same about delivering a digital product. Finding a talented team and giving them the ingredients feels like all that you need to do to create your perfect cocktail.

Unfortunately, that isn't the case.

Think about what happens when you're sitting at the bar watching the mixologist do their work. The processes they follow all seem simple enough. The measures are the same each time, the ingredients all match up, and yet you can end up with a different experience than the one you had at the last bar you visited. I actually test this out regularly myself. I love a good "Old-Fashioned." This cocktail has a super simple recipe that involves sugar syrup, a couple of dashes of bitters, a little or more bourbon, a splash of water, flavorsome fresh orange slices, and my favorite, the infused Maraschino Cherry (sigh). Combine the ingredients, mix them, and you should have an old-fashioned. But I've had enough bad versions of this cocktail to know that having all of the ingredients is not the same as being able to successfully mix them into something spectacular!

Everything from the atmosphere a bar creates to the specific way the mixologist combines the ingredients, affects the end product. An extra shake there or a couple of missed steps here may be all that's needed to make the difference between a good cocktail and one that makes me never want to drink at that bar again! I have been to bars where they put the cocktail glass under a glass bowl and smoke charcoal or sage to infuse it, and I can tell you the recommended wait is salivating, teasing torture that adds to the pleasure.

My point here is that having all of the ingredients means nothing without that sprinkling of magic that allows you to deliver the result that a customer wants or, more importantly, needs. The process of making the cocktail is simple. The mix of skills and elements brought into the process allows the cocktail to stand out from everything else.

Think back to the story I shared about Tom Scarpello and Revology in Chapter One. The ingredients he mixed together sound logical enough. If you were in his position, you might deduce that you need those same ingredients. However, the reason Revology achieved the success that it did was that Tom was the perfect passionate mixologist. He didn't only have the ingredients. He had a very specific set of skills and some love for his work that made him the ideal person for blending those ingredients together to create amazing results.

The same goes for delivering a digital solution. Again, the general process is simple. It's all about coding, computing, pixels on a screen, software selection, data integration, configuration, and following methodological instructions to deliver a user experience. And yet, thousands of failed apps, websites, and software products out there don't deliver what users particularly want to taste over time. I believe this happens because technologists often don't take (or can't get, often because of their organization structures and tribes) what they need to learn from their prospective customers before they work on a solution. Often, I would say technologists don't listen as they already know what they want to do by some higher divine power or telepathy, and it sometimes feels that whatever it is, it is definitely not what their predecessors delivered! Contrast this with a cocktail bar I choose to frequent because they can make a good old-fashioned. Over time, the mixologist will learn more about me, which enables them to hone their process to deliver something even better. This "knowledge worker" is also actually allowed and trusted to talk to customers.

Recently, I was at the Nai Harn Hotel in Phuket, Thailand, and read this:

"SIGNATURE COCKTAILS CREATED BY BAR LEGEND SALIM KHOURY"

Salim Khoury, the former Head Barman of the famous American Bar at the Savoy Hotel in London, visited The Nai Harn every year since our re-opening in 2015 and spent one month working with and training our team in the fine art of mixology. Salim joined the American Bar in 1969 and worked there for more than 30 years before he was appointed the 10th Head Barman in 2003. During his illustrious career, he also won the UK "Barman of the Year" award in 1992 with his cocktail tribute to Princess Diana, the "Blushing Monarch." To celebrate his association with The Nai Harn, Salim Khoury created a number of signature cocktails for our guests to enjoy. Sadly, Salim passed away after a short illness in June 2021. It is now our turn to celebrate his life by dedicating a special edition of his favorite cocktail, the Martini, to him. Stirred, of course—never shaken!!!

The American Bar at the Savoy Hotel is a great cocktail bar with the added emotional experience of history (and my emotional connection of getting engaged in the kitchens of the Savoy). I am pleased to say the Old Fashioned there and at the Nai Harn are both top drawer. However, there were other significant messages in that text:

- **Tenure**: learning the lessons of what you have delivered over time, reaping the feedback
- Building upon what went before: not always throwing away, making progress on sure foundations of knowledge and experience of others
- Pride and pleasure in outcomes
- Sustainability and earned progression
- Aspiration and craft.

Let's now take a broader view of how to achieve digital success.

You must properly frame both the problem and the opportunity before you start work on a digital solution.

This chapter focuses on how you can do that, thereby enabling you to develop a process that delivers a digital product successfully. You have to want to see technology and Digital as a non-commodity to achieve success.

The Four Easy Steps

Let's start by looking at the four easy steps for delivering digital. If you've been paying attention so far, you can already guess that these steps are not all that goes into it, at least not at the level I'm about to describe them. There are many almost religious ideologies for technology delivery with their own activists and adherents. Still, ultimately, these basic four steps serve as the recipe for delivering a digital solution that you will always follow.

Step #1—Discovery

Returning to our cocktail metaphor, a mixologist must first learn what they need to make before they start creating a cocktail. If they don't, they'll likely end up making something the customer doesn't enjoy, leading to losing that customer in the process.

Seems so simple, right?

And yet, so many companies fail to undertake this discovery period when building their digital solutions. What often happens is that somebody comes up with an idea, thinks it sounds good in their head, and then gets to work on it without taking the time to find out if the idea is actually what the market wants. To borrow a concept from earlier in the book, they make the biggest mistake that so many humans make:

They believe that everybody thinks like they do.

If they think an idea is good, they allow their own biases to lead them to the decision that *everybody* will or can be eventually influenced to agree with them. Unfortunately, the sad fact is that this is rarely the case. Making the mistake of believing that everybody thinks as you do is often the first step towards doing something in an organization that costs a lot of money and delivers little in the way of results. We can even argue that this approach is the exact opposite of the outside-in approach we aim for. The biases will naturally be due to marination in the inside-out context. A lack of discovery means you don't understand whether there's a need for your product, have data to learn from, or options to consider. And if you don't know if there's a need, there's no way to consider said need ahead of the product you're developing.

And so, our first step is to discover, with some honest, humble investigation.

Discover what the customer needs and focus your development on what you find. Otherwise, you're just making a random cocktail, hoping somebody somewhere will pay for it and hopefully drink it without buyer's remorse or a hangover.

Step #2—Research Ingredients

Once you know what the customer wants, you need to research the ingredients that will go into the end product. Our mixologist does this by learning about every cocktail available on the menu, ensuring they can quickly whip up the particular drink when asked.

For a digital solution, this research should obviously be more in-depth. When you know what the customer wants, you must, of course, research the specific technologies that will enable you to deliver the desired solution to them. The ingredients also go far beyond the tech into those aspects that help convey feeling remotely and digitally. The team you build, the skills each individual has, and even the equipment you use to develop the solution are also ingredients you must consider, and that will consciously or unconsciously influence the breadth of solution options considered and the bias within the decision making. The team selection and mix are vital. The best teams I have seen are open to engagement with customers and any other stakeholders. They are open to debate without agenda, and where there are not sufficient facts, then research and trial options are considered and enacted with open minds. Often, team selection can conflict with the hierarchy (e.g., some are too important to be involved but have control over approvals) or be functional/job title-based rather than considering the mix of skills and people for the problems or opportunities.

Step #3—Frame, Have Fun, and Experiment

Imagine you didn't ask for a specific cocktail at the bar. Instead, you give the mixologist a short list of the things you like and challenge them to come up with something that suits your tastes. What will follow is a period of experimentation where the mixologist "frames" the ingredients you describe and spends some time figuring out how to turn them into a tasty drink. Hopefully, they'll have a little fun along the way. But the key here is that they exercise their creative muscles, combined with their existing skills and experience, to develop a solution.

One key consideration of "framing" is scope. Imagine making a cocktail that you are not allowed to drink. How often has a digital project misused a definition of the V in MVP (Minimum Viable Product) to get away with inside-out designed solutions driven by a function fixing a symptom that impacts them? Personally, I prefer MSP (Minimum Sellable Product). If nobody outside the organization in their right mind would pay for the digital solution or service it provides, then… Well, you get the point. Don't forget the previous discourse about MVP being a cover up for a pin-the-tail-on-the-donkey approach to digital.

You will do this once you've gathered the ingredients for your digital product. The customer gives you an idea of what they want. You then start working on different recipes, experimenting with ideas, until you come up with something that "tastes" good using all senses.

Step #4—The Learn, Make, Test Cycle

Your experimentation will lead to a product prototype. What happens next?

You don't just release that prototype into the wild and expect to get a positive response. You test it, gain feedback on it, learn from that feedback, and implement it to improve the product. In our cocktail bar, this may involve the mixologist asking the customer to take a sip of the drink. They'll then get feedback and build on what they've created.

This cycle continues until the mixologist crafts the perfect cocktail for the customer based on making the customer feel comfortable enough to give honest feedback. And it's a cycle that you will follow in developing your digital solution.

The Journey to Reflective Competence

As you can see, the steps to follow in creating a digital solution are simple on paper. The challenge comes in following those steps to develop a viable solution. It's here where competence comes into play. In the case of our cocktail mixologist, competence comes from a combination of training and years of experience. However, this is a simplistic view of what it takes to develop true competence.

To develop competence, one must first recognize the areas where they're incompetent, allowing them to focus on those areas to develop their skills. In other words, we must become conscious of our competence, or lack thereof, before developing our solutions. This brings me to an organizational concept called the Conscious Competence Learning Model.

This model maps out the five stages of competence, which we can equate to the five stages you must go through to learn how to do something new. The five stages of the model are as follows:

- Unconscious Incompetence
- Conscious Incompetence

- Conscious Competence
- Unconscious Competence
- Reflective Competence.

Ultimately, the goal is always to move through these stages until you reach the level of Reflective Competence. I'll talk about what that means in a moment. First, it's important to note that the ideas I'm about to present here are nothing new, at least in the world of organization theory. Former Director of the Centre for Higher Education Practice at the Open University, David Baume, speaks at length about these concepts in some of his courses, as does Lorgene Mata. Some of their opinions, plus links to their research, can be found at https://www.businessballs.com/self-awareness/conscious-competence-learning-model/ if you'd like to read further on this subject.

As you read, you'll likely notice that you already know much of what I'm about to tell you about competence, even if you haven't formalized or structured these concepts in your head. With that in mind, let's jump into both the conscious and unconscious realms.

Stage #1—Unconscious Incompetence

We could call this stage a complete lack of awareness of both the skill area and the level of incompetence you may have in this area. In short, you don't even know that the area exists for you to improve on it. As such, you're also not aware that you have a deficiency in that area because, how could you? You don't even know the skill exists.

The danger with this stage is that unconscious incompetence can lead to your denying the relevance or usefulness of the skill in question. There's an element of arrogance at play here, as you may default to the thought process of, "If I don't know about it, then that must mean it isn't important."

That's a dangerous mindset to have in any organization setting. But when it comes to digital, it's especially hazardous as so much of what you may need to understand to complete a project could be completely new to you. Dismissing such skill areas outright means your project will not have the ingredients needed to bring it to fruition.

To move past this stage, you must become conscious of both the skill area and your lack of competence in it. This will then feed into the next stage.

Stage #2—Conscious Incompetence

Naturally, becoming aware of a skill area where you lack competence means you become conscious of that skill. However, understanding that the skill exists and actually developing it are two very different things. You're still deficient in this area, which means you're not able to use the skill in question. But the good news is that you're aware of both this deficiency and the relevance the skill has to your project. In some cases, this may mean that you're able to identify that a particular skill isn't needed for your project. In others, your consciousness shows you that there's a knowledge gap that you need to fill, either through direct learning, training your people, or bringing somebody new into the fold.

If you decide that you need to improve your own competence in the identified skill, you will ideally begin with some measure of your level of incompetence. This allows you to determine what you need to do to build true competence, in addition to helping you commit to the learning process. Being able to map your journey from incompetence to competence allows you to create milestones that serve as motivators as you move toward conscious competence.

If you decide to bring someone new or a supplier into the project, you have a different set of risks, including not really being competent to interview or determine whether the supplier competence exists at a depth beyond the pitch deck.

Stage #3—Conscious Competence

Many see this stage as the ideal outcome of learning, though we'll soon discover that it isn't the case.

Here, you are conscious of the skill area and have actively worked to develop your competence to the point where you're able to execute a skill or perform a task reliably well. In our cocktail example, this could mean that our person has identified that they make a terrible old-fashioned, so they've practiced constantly until they get it right consistently.

However, the skill doesn't come naturally to the person at this stage. You will still need to concentrate to perform the skill, even though you can do it without aid. It's not yet second nature, which means you may not be able to consider yourself a complete expert. For a good example, imagine that you're learning how to play the guitar. You reach the stage of conscious competence when you're able to play some songs while concentrating. Your eyes are always on the fretboard, and you need to keep track of the rhythm in your head. However, when you watch virtuosic players on stage, you can see that they rarely need to even look at their fretboards to play well.

The skill seems to come naturally to them, which is a perception that can only exist because they have trained to a level above conscious competence!

Still, being at this stage means you're able to perform a skill and demonstrate it to others. You may not be able to teach it just yet, but you're at least capable of doing so. In our next stage, we see the difference between an at-home guitarist and the virtuoso on stage.

Stage 4—Unconscious Competence

At first glance, the name of this stage implies a person is naturally good at something without even realizing that something is actually a skill. For example, somebody may have the gift of gab without realizing that being a good speaker could be relevant for so many careers.

But that isn't what unconscious competence is all about.

Instead, this stage is more about the guitar virtuoso I mentioned in the previous stage. When you achieve unconscious incompetence, you are so practiced in a skill that it moves into the unconscious part of your brain. It becomes second nature to you, which means you're able to perform the skill with little to no thought.

Perhaps a better example of this stage is the progression you experience when you're learning to ride a bike. Think back to when you were a kid and how much of a struggle it was to figure out how to balance while on your bike. You were conscious of everything, from how fast you were peddling to the position of your hands on the handlebars. But over time, and with a lot of practice, everything about riding a bike became natural to you. In fact, it feels so natural that if you don't ride for years, you'll still be right at home when you finally hop back on a bike. Hence, the expression "it's like riding a bike" when we talk about using a skill that we haven't used for a while.

Other examples may include reading, driving, knitting, and so many other tasks that we're able to do unconsciously with enough practice. These are all skills that can become so ingrained in your unconscious mind that you may even be able to execute them while doing something else, as you might have seen granny doing when she knitted while watching TV when you were a kid.

The challenge with this level of competence is that you may end up losing the ability to explain *how* you've reached this level. This can make teaching especially difficult. You're so good at what you do that you don't even have to think about it, which means you have to try and step back into your consciousness to teach others. It's this challenge that has led to much debate about what the fifth stage of the Conscious Confidence Learning Model should be.

Stage #5—Reflective Competence

Before we jump into this final stage, I want to preface it by acknowledging the debate that exists on what should follow unconscious competence. Some argue that complacency is the next stage. In other words, you become so good at something that you no longer respect the true level of skill required to execute the task. This is a valid next stage in some cases. It also highlights the need for continued learning and development of a skill.

Driving offers us an excellent example of complacency taking form. When you first pass your test, you're likely still in the conscious competence stage. You can drive well but have to think about it as you do. Over time, everything you do in the car becomes automatic to the point where you develop unconscious competence. But in doing so, you open yourself up to developing bad habits through complacency. And perhaps it's one of these bad habits that leads to even the most extremely competent drivers occasionally having accidents.

So, the claim that complacency should be the fifth stage of this model has some credibility. However, accepting this stage also means accepting that people put no safeguards in place to protect themselves from complacency or that they're somehow so unaware of complacency that it will affect them no matter what.

I don't believe that is the case, which is why I much prefer the idea that the fifth stage of this model is one called Reflective Competence.

We can best define this as being conscious of your unconscious competence. This sounds like an excellent tongue twister, but the idea is that you develop the ability to examine your unconscious competence from the outside. You dig into it to understand the models, theories, and beliefs that allow you to execute a task seemingly at will.

> As you work to understand what lies beneath your level of competence, you develop the ability to inform others about what you do and how you do it. As such, you enter a stage where you're not only able to perform, you're able to teach!

The journey to reflective confidence is one you should encourage all of the mixologists in your organization to undertake. The goal here is to spread the concept of mixology, i.e., the ability to deliver on all customer expectations, as a philosophy that is ingrained into your organization's culture. By encouraging your mixologists to dig into what makes them so special, you also equip them with the ability to teach others. Eventually, you end up with a team of unconsciously competent mixologists, many of whom have achieved reflective competence that is tested and honed through a variety of contexts and customers.

With a team operating at this level of competence, you can feel more confident in your organization's ability to frame a project and execute the fulsome integration of "outside-in" designed outcomes via sustainable choices of ingredients to bring that project to completion.

Discovering the Knowns and Unknowns

During a news briefing in 2002, the United States' former Secretary of Defense, Donald Rumsfeld, found himself getting grilled about the nature of intelligence reports that led the US into war with Iraq. It was during this briefing that Rumsfeld came out with a gem of a quote:

> *"There are known knowns. These are things we know that we know. There are known unknowns. That is to say, there are things that we know we don't know. But there are also unknown unknowns. There are things we don't know we don't know."*

Interestingly, Rumsfeld was widely ridiculed for this quote (I remember a scene in a Michael Moore movie lambasting it) even though it makes perfect sense normally. We will stay out of the politics and morality about who knew what and when about weapons of mass destruction and treat it as an interesting quote.

Similar to the conscious and unconscious competence issues I mentioned earlier, there are different levels of knowing inside your organization. Building on what Rumsfeld said, there are four that are relevant to you:

- Unknown Unknowns
- Unknown Knowns
- Known Unknowns
- Known Knowns.

Perhaps this is best illustrated with a diagram called Johari Window, which was earlier developed by psychologists Joseph Luft and Harrington Ingham.

	Known to self	Not known to self
Known to others	Arena	Blind Spot
Not known to others	Facade	Unknown

The idea behind this model was to help people evaluate how they think about themselves when compared to how others might think about them. In this example, a Blind Spot is a thing we don't see in ourselves but others see in us.

The most interesting thing about this concept is that it also applies to your organization, particularly when it comes to digital design thinking. Sticking with the Blind Spot example, there are likely things (perhaps gaps) that others, such as your customers or suppliers, see in your organization that you don't see at all. The question now is how can we apply all of these knowns and unknowns to our digital designs? Importantly, it should not be a surprise to people and teams that there are more blind spots in digital, given the pace of change and a customer's ease in checking our competitors dispassionately.

I will explore each of the four levels I mentioned earlier in a moment. But as you read this, I want you to remember that exploring all levels of known and unknown allows you to make your problem space larger. While this may not sound attractive at first, doing so also means your solution space grows. The goal here is to bring to the surface all of the available knowledge, which allows you to create a digital solution that serves the needs of your customers while accounting for every possible issue along the way. With gaps, it is also important to understand their materiality to customers based on lifetime value or other metrics of importance to you. As a simple illustrative example, for convenience, I try not to visit supermarkets that don't sell Vimto, and I am happy to shop somewhere with many other gaps, but not this gap. Whether I matter or not to the supermarkets I don't visit is up to them. But if they don't know what their gaps and the impacts of these gaps are, then they are designing their organization around Unconscious Incompetence with regard to their addressable market, which isn't sensible in aggregate.

This is also your weakest moment in a digital transformation journey when someone already has a solution framed before the full set of questions and analyzed data are known; perhaps a helpful SaaS provider or copying a competitor or a recommendation to someone important.

With that in mind, let's jump into our unknowns and knowns. If you do really know everything then do skip ahead.

Level #1—Unknown Unknowns

These are the trickiest pieces of information to unearth simply because you don't know that you don't know something. Think of it in similar terms to unconscious incompetence. In that case, you're not competent in a skill because you don't know it exists or that it could be relevant to your project. In the case of unknown unknowns, there is information floating around out there that you don't even know exists. And because you don't know it exists, you can't actively go out and seek it.

You wouldn't even know what you're looking for.

It all gets a little confusing.

But the trick to unearthing unknown unknowns is to approach your project with an open mind. For example, you can hold interviews with a sufficiently diverse mix of potential customers or users where you ask them what they would look for in a digital solution. Go in with no assumptions and listen to what these people have to say. You may uncover a pattern of user needs that you didn't even know existed before the interviews occurred. In doing so, you find an unknown unknown that can serve as an opportunity for you to better understand a problem so you can come up with a solution.

Level #2—Unknown Knowns

We can almost compare this level to unconscious competence in the sense that unknown knowns represent information that you have without realizing it. Floating around somewhere in your brain (or in your team) is a piece of the puzzle that you can use to build a better project. The problem is that you're not consciously aware of this knowledge, as it hasn't come to the fore during your design phase. That means you can't leverage it despite the fact that you know it.

Again, it all sounds very confusing. But think about it like this. Have you ever sat down for a brainstorming session with your team and come up with a bunch of ideas that you hadn't even considered when going into the session? This is the perfect environment for uncovering your unknown knowns. Somebody may say something seemingly tangential, only for another person in the room to bounce off that thought to bring related knowledge to the surface. Somebody else bounces off that knowledge until you end up with fully formed ideas that you wouldn't have uncovered on your own.

So, we see that collaboration is the key to finding our unknown knowns. Perhaps our biggest takeaway here is that your design team has hidden value that you need to find a way to extract when designing your digital solution. Obviously, you also need to design your design team to have a mix of outside and inside perspectives as well as a diversity of thought, skills, and experience to avoid groupthink.

Level #3—Known Unknowns

Finally, we enter into the more conscious level of our knowns and unknowns. There are plenty of obvious examples of known unknowns that can apply to your project. For example, you may wish to develop an app that requires a specific API, data set, AI model, architectural pattern, or programming language that your team isn't familiar with. In this case, you know exactly what you don't know, which means you can take steps to fill the knowledge gap, conscious of the long-term cost/benefits related to the decision. Or, consider how you design the user experience for your solution. Typically, this involves creating a bunch of sketches that show how users flow from one area of the solution to the next. Again, this is stuff you know you need to create. But until you start building those diagrams and running them through the filter of your customers and team, you don't know exactly how your solution will fit together.

Your known unknowns are really ideas that come from your existing knowledge. You're aware of what your project may need and can use those ideas to form hypotheses. However, there's still a lot of information that you don't have, which is why you enter into a research period to learn as much as possible.

Level #4—Known Knowns

These are your facts about the project. It's the stuff that you know exists, you know is relevant, and you know how to leverage to bring the project to fruition. Through your known knowns, you can create more knowledge, provide yourself with a base for further research, and approach design challenges from a range of perspectives.

But here's the rub:

Your known knowns will typically fit into conventional knowledge or thinking and are obviously unconsciously skewed by inside-out thinking. This means that creating a solution based only on your known knowns means you end up with something that's typical of everything else available. In other words, your digital product won't feel unique because it just leverages what already exists to create something that is likely already available.

The trick with your known knowns is to use them as a base for extrapolation. Your aim is to create something unique and valuable, using your known knowns as a foundation and then exploring other levels of knowledge to discover what your digital project needs to make it stand out.

Ultimately, this feeds back into what I discussed at the beginning of this section. To create an amazing digital solution, you can't rely on only the things that you know. Take our cocktail mixologist as an example. He knows the ins and outs of every single cocktail on his menu, and he can serve every one of them up without issue.

But if he has a customer who requests something different or wants the mixologist to come up with a cocktail based on the customer's preferences, that's when we slip out of the known knowns territory. The mixologist has to explore the unknowns (what the customer typically enjoys, how he can mix these ingredients to create something new) while using his existing knowledge base as a foundation for the cocktail he'll end up creating.

If we think of your digital solution as this cocktail, your known knowns are the ingredients that you know you need to include. Everything else is stuff that you have to discover along the way during the design process. Your customer research, brainstorming sessions, and design documentation help you to uncover knowledge, both known and unknown, that contributes to the creation of a unique digital solution.

One of my personal maxims is to be judicious as to where and when to innovate, i.e., when is standard good enough, and where should the novelty be created to address the customer need, differentiate organization strategy, etc. This is yet another twist in the skill of mixology.

The Service Design Philosophy

In the past, we had a clear distinction between goods and services. Goods were tangible objects, such as pens, clothes, and food.

Services were the less tangible things that did not result in ownership of a product, such as medical treatment or public transportation. For decades, the line between these two types of products was clear.

But that isn't the case anymore. And the perfect example of this is the SaaS (Software as a Service) organization model. With SaaS, the customer receives a tangible product that they're able to use for something, be it for entertainment, organization purposes, or anything else. However, the SaaS model means that the customer doesn't own the software, and even with some subscriptions, they lose some rights to their data. They typically pay a subscription fee to gain access to a license to use it. If they stop paying the subscription, they can no longer use the software. Furthermore, if they break the conditions of the service agreement they signed up for, they can no longer use the software. So, is the service a product?

The lines have blurred as services have grown in sophistication. And this leads us into needing to follow the principles of service design to provide our customers with what they need from our digital solutions.

In 1982, a banker named G. Lynn Shostack coined the term "service design" in an article published in *Harvard Organization Review*. Her idea was that organizations need to better understand how their behind-the-scenes systems and processes relate to and interact with one another. In doing so, the organization would move away from the siloing effect that leads to departments being responsible for individual pieces of a product or service. Instead, all of the pieces of an organization should join together and work in harmony to create a service that reacts to market needs and opportunities.

Again, we can see this in the SaaS model, which allows for constant updates and iterations of the base service as user needs change and the market evolves.

In essence, Shostack argued that organizations tended to overlook their internal processes in favor of focusing on customer outputs. The espoused converse irony is that by overlooking what's going on inside your organization, your customer output and quality tend to weaken. You end up trying to fit a bunch of individual pieces of a puzzle together, with no coordination between teams, to produce something you think customers will purchase. If we come back to our mixologist, this is the equivalent of dumping a bunch of random ingredients on a table and telling the mixologist to create a cocktail. They'll be able to come up with *something* for the customer. But, with so many disparate pieces to try to mix together, there's no guarantee that the cocktail will be what the customer actually wants. In organizations, the ingredients are also structural or process choices that can create an ideological jarring with the outside world—particularly through the way that digital exposes the internals of an organization.

With this in mind, service design exists to enable organizations to focus on their internal processes. Nielsen Norman Group provides us with a perfect definition in its 2017 article, *Service Design 101*:

> *"Service design is the activity of planning and organizing an organization's resources (people, props, and processes) to (1) directly improve the employee's experience, and (2) indirectly, the customer's experience."*

The same article also offers an example of a restaurant to demonstrate service design in action. Any restaurant has a host of employees, from waiters and on-floor managers to chefs, cooks, and even bartenders. The quality of the service the restaurant provides depends on how well each of these individuals works together to create an experience. Waiters must quickly communicate what diners want to the chefs, who then create the dishes in a set time to be sent back out. Everything, from the people involved to the ingredients used to the décor, training, and menu, plays a part in creating the designing experience. The key here is that none of these parts act individually. All aspects of the restaurant's internal processes are brought together to form an exceptional customer experience.

In creating your digital solution, understanding and leveraging service design are two keys to building something customers will appreciate, engage with, and value.

The Core Components of Service Design

There are three core components of the service design philosophy:

1. People
2. Props
3. Processes.

The People component refers both to the people inside your organization who create and operate the service *and* the users of that service. It also incorporates any organization partners you have, such as investors or technology suppliers.

Props refer to both the physical and digital artifacts required to deliver the service. For example, our mixologist has his ingredients, cocktail glasses, shaker, bar, and so on. In your digital solution, your props may include your website, blogs, customer database, order database, social media pages, and any digital files and downloads you provide to your users.

Finally, the Processes are any procedures or workflows you have in place that allow your customers to use your service. Again, this refers to both the internal and external. Let's take withdrawing money from an ATM as an example. The customer-facing process involves inserting a card, entering a PIN, and selecting the amount of money you wish to withdraw. Behind the scenes, there are a bunch of other processes, all automated, that deliver on the requests the customer makes.

> *In successfully understanding and combining these three core elements, you successfully use service design to provide something exceptional to the customers.*

How Does Service Design Differ From Designing a Service?

Service Design and Designing a Service are not the same things, with the differences going far beyond the flipping around of words. When designing a service, you focus on the customer's journey. That means covering all the touchpoints the user hits when receiving that service. However, as discussed, service design focuses more on your internal processes, with the effects on the user being a by-product of good service design.

Ultimately, service design encourages agility within your organization because it forces you to focus on how your internal processes affect both your employees and customers. You have to adapt your processes constantly to stay competitive in an ever-evolving market. A focus on service design enables this adaptability, though that is far from the only benefit.

Service design also enables you to consider everybody involved in the delivery of a service. You move away from only thinking about the customer and towards examining the impact your choices have on your employees and their ability to deliver the service. This allows you to design ideal human interactions based on both what your customers need and how to best organize your processes to deliver on those needs in a way that satisfies employees and internal stakeholders. As such, the service design philosophy also involves transitioning into a more relationship-driven organization model.

> *Ultimately, we come back to the core benefit of service design, which is that it allows your organization to embrace changes in the market.*

We are at risk of running afoul of a semantic overload here. This flipping between Service Design and Design a Service can be confusing even in this chapter. The reality is that one feeds or interacts with the other.

So, let's simplify things a little.

The key to Service Design is to follow these guiding principles:

- Design how the inside operating model can deliver it.

- Always avoid trying to design something that you know can't be delivered.

However, without Design a Service, then what is the goal or needs of the Service Design?

Finally, we also see how Design a Service helps us to avoid the inside-out approach that we have previously discussed. With inside-out, the focus is always on the product, without any consideration for whether the market needs that product.

Service Design feeds into the outside-in model, allowing you to foster digital innovation and enable the shift to a more agile form of delivery and, ultimately, deliver what your customers want. It can give you a start, that is, what capability is easily digitizable (often under the "self-service" label), but it is no substitute for

Designing a Service that customers would actually like and pay for as the primary objective.

People, Inertia, and Service Design

Let's hone in on the "People" aspect of service design for a moment. You can have all of the Props and Processes in place to design a service, only to be let down by the People you rely on.

Why does this happen?

There are many reasons. However, one of the most pressing is inertia within your organization. Inertia is a psychological concept that has a direct effect on how your people behave when they're presented with new challenges, such as Designing a Service. When inertia is in full force, you will find that your people do everything they can, consciously or otherwise, to maintain the status quo of how they've always operated.

The change will be met with resistance and a lack of desire. Your people may drag their feet, complain about how the "old way" worked better, and generally show a lack of ambition or fear as you attempt to spearhead transformation. Inertia, ultimately, can kill any attempts you make to adapt your organization to the demands of the modern market. This makes it a key challenge to overcome, not only in terms of service design, but in terms of creating an agile and adaptable organization.

I won't dig too much into the concept here as we'll be looking at inertia, its causes, its effects, and what you can do about it in a later chapter. For now, it's enough to know that inertia is a key people challenge that you will need to overcome to leverage service design to the fullest.

Service Design and Your People

So, we can see from all of this that your people are a vital component of the Service Design philosophy. If you fail to consider the human element, Service Design will always fall down. As such, you need to engage in the fourth of our easy steps from earlier in the chapter.

Do you remember what that step was?

The Learn, Make, Test Cycle.

The goal here is to better understand your people (your ingredients) and how you can mix their talents together to create a digital service (your cocktail).

In an article published in a 2012 edition of *McKinsey Quarterly*, authors John Device, Michael Zea, and Shyam Lal introduce three questions that they believe organization leaders should ask before introducing any new services to the market. These questions are designed to help you better understand your people, and I share them here with my own insights.

Question #1—How Human Is Our Service?

This question is all about determining how your internal processes impact your customers. The aim here is to determine how customers form their opinions of your service and, in the process, figure out what you can do internally to provide a better service to make those opinions more favorable.

Device et al. give the example of a cable TV provider in their article. This provider had developed a reputation for poor service that it hoped to improve. Its first step was to examine the characteristics of the most important interactions it has with customers and the phone calls it makes when initiating a new service, to identify the pain points customers dealt with during these interactions. For example, the organization found these calls often included "dead" periods, where customers felt like the organization was wasting their time.

While this seems like a customer-focused approach, it actually revealed problems in the cable organization's internal processes. That "dead" time shouldn't be happening. The fact that it is means there is an internal process problem. By fixing that problem, the service provided to the customer becomes more human and less frustrating.

So, this question encourages you to examine the customer experience in the context of how your internal processes create that experience. You start to think about what makes your customers tick and what they expect from your service. This allows you to hone in on the weaknesses inherent in your internal processes, which creates the opportunity to turn those weaknesses into strengths. You may even be able to identify new service offerings by just listening to your customers and focusing on making your interactions with them more human.

Question #2—How Economic Is Our Service?

The *McKinsey* article goes on to offer an example of a rental car organization that discovered that its "value" segment customers experienced more anxiety when searching for a car in the lot than their "premium" customers. Further examination of this tendency revealed the likely cause was that "value" customers tended to rent cars infrequently. As a result, they weren't as aware of the processes involved.

The solution?

Implement a "pick any car" system that simplifies the process, both for employees and renters. It's outside-in again! The need gets confronted before the product. By servicing the need, in this case reducing anxiety for "value" segment customers, the rental car organization can provide a service that satisfies its clients.

And that example brings us to our next question of how economical your service is. Every organization has to make trade-offs when delivering a service to the public. Unless you somehow have access to an unlimited pot of cash (and if you do, feel free to tell me where it is), you will need to consider your budget when creating a service.

How much will building this service cost?
What are the expected revenue benefits?
Are there any revenue benefits at all?

These are all questions that fit under the economic umbrella. In the case of the car rental organization, the switch to a "pick any car" process was economic as well as human. It simplified the old system, made it easier for customers to find a car, and, crucially, meant that employees didn't have to dedicate as much of their time helping anxious customers. Again, we see the system design philosophy of improving processes for your people with the goal of creating a better experience for your customers.

However, the point of this question is that you will need to weigh your financial resources up against any service solution you propose. In some cases, the ideal solution won't be economically viable, at least in your organization's current state. Forging ahead with it may lead to internal improvements but can come at a major cost for the organization as a whole. Your goal is to find a compromise that allows you to develop an effective process without creating financial hardship.

Question #3—Can Our People Scale It Up?

So, our first two questions allow us to create a service that is both economically viable and takes our customers into consideration.

Better yet, our focus is still on developing internal processes that improve the relationships we have with our employees on top of those we have with customers.

But it's with our third question that we fully focus on the needs of our employees.

Can they take the process you've created and scale it up to the point where they can deliver on it consistently in all areas of the organization? In other words, can your people adopt the process, adapt to new requirements, automate where relevant, and execute on it?

Creating new processes is only one aspect of service delivery. If your people don't have the organizational capacity required to execute those processes, the whole thing falls down. This is where our cycle of Learn, Make, Test really comes into play. When creating a new service, you typically aim to introduce it on a small scale. This is your testing period where you get to see if the process can work when it involves a small number of your employees.

If it doesn't, you obviously have to go back to the drawing board to make a new process. But if it does, that isn't the green light for you to implement at scale. Instead, it simply means the process passed one test. From there, you have to go back, examine what you learned from that test, and determine whether the process will work when implemented widely throughout the organization.

Your Organization Is a Living Organism

It's all starting to sound a little complex or deep, isn't it?

What all of this information about shifting to the service design philosophy shows us is that our traditional view of the organization as a machine where the humans have not quite yet been replaced is outdated. Your organization is not a conveyor belt designed to pump out the same product over and over again. It is a living and breathing organism filled with processes, systems, and people that influence your success.

Think of your organization in terms of evolutionary science. Building an unchanging machine is no longer the goal. Like all machines, it will eventually become outdated as the technology moves on and the needs of consumers change. Rather, you build an organism that's capable of adapting to rapidly changing environments created by changing consumer needs and the introduction of disruptive technologies. As automation in all its forms accelerates, the design and oversight skills required for this organism also need to change. An organism needs to be healthy to thrive and change.

In a word, your organization needs to become, to use the cliche, AGILE!

A 2018 *McKinsey and Organization* report titled *The five trademarks of agile organizations* focuses on this need to transition to the agile model. The report mentioned a survey the organization conducted that involved 2,500 organization leaders. That survey aimed to determine how many of those leaders believed they had successfully conducted an agile transformation. In other words, how many successfully made the move from machine to organism?

The survey showed that most organization leaders were in pursuit of agility, but very few had managed to achieve it. In fact, fewer than 10% of respondents claimed to have completed an agility transformation at the performance-unit level. This is despite the fact that 75% of the leaders said that achieving organizational agility is either their top or a top-three priority.

The message here is that organization leaders at least recognize the need for agility, even if they've yet to achieve it. And I wouldn't be surprised if you fall into the same category as the 90% who have yet to achieve an agility transformation. With that in mind, I will dedicate this section of the chapter to defining the five characteristics of an agile organization before offering some ideas that may help you introduce agile at scale in your organization.

Let's jump into the traits!

Trait #1—A North Star

Think of your North Star as your purpose and vision, sitting high up in the sky and guiding your entire organization toward your destination. The purpose and vision are shared between you, your employees, and even your customers. And it is in following this

North Star that you're able to identify opportunities and allocate resources that enable you to seize them.

Agile organizations commit to more than providing value to customers, though this is still an important part of the equation. They will also seek to create value, both with and for other stakeholders. This includes employees, investors, and partners.

Trait #2—A Network of Teams

You may notice that we're seeing several of the tenets of service delivery seeping into agility here. This is especially the case when we focus on the need to develop a network of teams. In traditional organization models, our teams are often siloed away from one another. Even worse, they are often structured into ideological disciplines. Marketing has different goals than Sales, which has different goals than HR, and so on. The agile model encourages creating a network that all your teams are a part of.

In doing so, you both clearly outline roles and accountabilities while ensuring each team stays focused on the collective goal. The result is an organization where all of the core ingredients are successfully mixed into a tasty rather than nasty cocktail, and rather than said ingredients all sitting outside the glass and not interacting with one another and the customer looking on bemused that they have to stir, muddle and shake themselves.

Trait #3—Fast Learning and Decision Cycles

Remember the Learn, Make, Test cycle I've talked about many times in this chapter? It's that cycle that plays most directly into this trait. Agile organizations commit to experimentation and innovation, which means they're constantly testing new ideas and iterating on the delivered service based on what they learn.

This isn't to say that such organizations don't have a standardized way of working. Agile does not mean creating a free-for-all environment where employees do whatever they feel like and somehow magically produce results. Instead, the model is all about encouraging rather than throttling creativity while taking all relevant project constraints into account in delivery. The focus lies both on performance and action, leading to an ever-evolving organism that learns quickly and makes rapid decisions based on what it learns from the environment.

Trait #4—A Strong People Model

People are the heart of the agile model, just as they are the key to effective service delivery. Agile organizations focus on developing internal (and external) communities. The leaders in these organizations aim to empower employees, rather than acting as looming overlords who bark directions and expect others to follow. With an agile organization, you serve as a motivator and empowerment expert. You encourage your people to take full ownership of their work and have confidence that they will pull your organization in the direction of your vision and purpose.

Your people are at the center of your organization. Without them, the enterprise will collapse. By empowering your people, you ignite their passion and create a community that employees are excited to be a part of.

A key area to examine is that of rewards for the right outcomes rather than based on the hierarchy of roles.

Trait #5—Enabling Technology

In the traditional organization model, technology is seen as little more than a supporting player. It's the crew member behind the scenes that makes your movie possible.

It's a tool. A giant hammer you use to smash a nail into the wood.

But tech is so much more than this in the agile mode. With agile, you aim to seamlessly integrate your technology into every aspect of your organization, making it as much a part of what you do as the people who use the tech. Your technology is what enables you to react quickly to changing environments, and it provides you with the means to unlock and add value to your service.

Making the Shift From Traditional to Agile

Now that we understand the traits of an agile organization, it's time to focus on how you can make the shift from a traditional model to an agile one. How do you make the move from machine to organism? The challenge here is that so many of your old practices are ingrained into your organizational structure. For example, consider your current thinking in terms of your accounting and finances. You likely have a system of financial governance in place that creates a stop/start workflow inside your organization that can destroy your velocity. The organization is in flow as you come up with an idea and start to develop a design around it. But, at some point, the financial questions need to be asked, which typically means the finance department stands directly in the flow, bringing it to a complete halt.

This is emblematic of an organization where the employees have to guess what your customers may want. In this example, Finance steps in to determine how the new idea may drive return on investment, which moves the focus away from how the customer wallet should be the thing driving that investment. Ultimately, the goal is to create a structure where you analyze at the side without disrupting the flow of ideas and development that leads to the creation of a digital service. And what's more, you need to do this at scale to create a truly agile organization.

How?

Your first step will often be to make your planning and budgeting processes more flexible. As with any budgeting model, the focus will remain on figuring out how to use your limited resources to provide the best possible service to your customers. However, the budgeting model must be flexible enough to respond quickly to changes. A process needs to be in place to allow your financing team to constantly assess your organization's priorities, allowing it to budget appropriately, without getting in the way of the flow of work.

This leads us to three best practices that people and teams involved with agile use to determine planning and budgets:

- Aim to fund tangible and long-lived products ahead of projects that introduce discrete, and often imperceptible, features into your service. This allows you to create clear definitions of what success looks like, enabling project managers to determine which tasks take priority based on what they deliver to your customers.

- Move away from the model where the finance department allocates funding on a calendar, perhaps on an annual basis. The digital environment changes far too rapidly for you to be able to safely assume that the priorities you had at the beginning of the year will remain priorities for the rest of the year. New customer needs and the introduction of disruptive technologies can change the course of your organization. Sticking to an annual funding model restricts your ability to adapt to these environmental changes. Aim to allocate funds more frequently, focusing on continuous analysis of business cases to determine which areas deserve more funding and which can be deprioritized.

- Develop a stronger funding feedback loop in which you receive real data on the performance of different organization areas based on the investment they've received. Again, this comes down to analyzing how current work proceeds based on the goals set for each area of work. This analysis allows you to make informed decisions about where to allocate funding in the future based on the metrics you select.

Ultimately, the transition to agile requires a change in mindset that must run throughout your entire organization. When you operate a machine, you get a machine's output. Your product will be consistent, and every process inside your organization will be rigid. And this will be fine for as long as the machine can deliver what the customers want. The problem comes when the machine becomes outdated due to the introduction of new technologies or changes in the market.

A machine cannot evolve.
An agile organism can.

By becoming agile, you introduce flexibility into your organizational model, allowing you to adapt to environmental changes. When developing a digital service, which is what we're really focusing on here, that flexibility is what prevents your organization from stagnating.

Agile is of course dead?

Many of you have just read the last section with a range of emotions, such as "We tried Agile, and it failed," or "We can't afford a proper multi-disciplinary team," or "Agile is insane—with the idea of no promises in terms of final budget or milestones," etc. I guess I could write another book on the philosophical problems Agile methodology evangelists.

However, rather than forcing me to tackle such a tedious task, please just re-read the sections on Silver Bullets and Reflective Competence. If you want a debate, then come sit with me in a cocktail bar, sip an Old Fashioned with me, and I will partake in the righting of wrongs that is best done amongst comrades on barstools.

Of course, agility cannot die, but you can bury it if you think that is a good move and prefer the alternative in this technological era. Methods, of course, die all the time and kill the minds of many victims through boredom and other tactics.

Creating Collective Ambition—The Glue and the Grease

I'd like to revisit the very first trait of an agile organization— having a North Star.

Think of your North Star as the purpose you create within your organization. It's here where we see even more of the outside-in concepts that I introduced in Chapter One come into play. Your purpose derives from your understanding of what your customers want. To fulfill that purpose, you must unite your people behind a collective ambition. Purpose comes first and it informs everything you do afterward.

In 2011, MIT senior lecturer Douglas A. Ready and Harvard Organization School assistant professor Emily Truelove collaborated on an article called *The Power of Collective Ambition*. Published in *Harvard Organization Review*, the article outlined how the duo had studied companies from various industries for three years to learn about the role that "purpose" played in allowing organizations to bounce back from the Global Financial Crisis (GFC) of 2008. The pair outlined the elements of what they called "collective ambition" and introduced a concept they called *The Glue and the Grease.*

They talk about how shaping a collective organization ambition is about more than sharing an inspiring story. The aim is to foster internal engagement as a means to achieve an end—making the organization's purpose personal. The idea is that shaping your collective ambition allows you to strengthen the glue that binds the disparate areas of your organization together. But running parallel to this is the need to use the grease to enable change initiatives that encompass the entire organization. The article explains these two concepts in more detail using the examples of Standard Chartered Bank (SCB) and Four Seasons Hotels.

The Glue

SCB was fortunate enough to already have a strong purpose heading into that GFC. Its purpose was to maintain a positive presence for all stakeholders. And this purpose fed into the long-term vision of becoming the world's foremost international bank, particularly in the African, Asian, and Middle Eastern territories. So, SCB had a large group of employees who understood why their work had a purpose. The problem was that the bank struggled to communicate this purpose to the rest of the world, making it difficult to show people what made it unique.

In 2009, SCB's CEO, Peter Sands, decided that this needed to change. He created a task force that would spend months traveling the world to meet with customers, employees, shareholders, and every other stakeholder the bank could identify. This effort revealed a common pattern in the perception that stakeholders from diverse backgrounds had of the bank:

It was in it for the long haul.

Bear in mind that this was in the wake of the GFC, when many global banks were pulling out of certain territories. SCB's vision of being the world's best international bank led to it staying where other banks might leave. And to many consumers, this led to the impression that the bank would stick with them during the good times and bad. Encapsulating this perception, a senior executive from SCB's Southeast Asia territory said:

> *"Our local connections are very deep, in part because we make a big effort to develop local talent and also because we've been in our markets so much longer than other multi-nationals. It is not uncommon for me to meet a customer who says, 'You gave my grandfather a loan 50 years ago, and you've stood by my family organization in good and bad times. We wouldn't go to another bank.'"*

In other words, SCB's commitment to its vision led to it taking actions that strengthened the glue binding the organization to its customers and other stakeholders. The result is that these stakeholders stick with the organization through thick and thin, just as the bank stuck with them. In your case, it's important to think about how your purpose binds others to your organization. What makes them stick around? How do they engage with your organization, its purpose, and your service? And how can you avoid the types of actions that weaken the glue, leading to people coming loose?

The Grease

Strengthening the glue means little if the process doesn't result in positive action. That's what former Four Seasons CEO Kathleen Taylor discovered when she assumed her leadership role in 2010. Like SCB, her first action was to create a task force of executives who traveled the globe to speak to guests, stakeholders, and employees about the organization. The findings showed that employees enjoyed a shared sense of purpose and guests valued the hotel chain's dedication to a luxury experience.

The challenge came in taking these findings from the theoretical stage and turning them into something more practical. While the task force helped to show the glue was strong, collective ambition was not yet achieved because no everyday solutions were coming from the findings.

Identifying this issue, Taylor developed a framework with a bias for action. This fed into the creation of a plan that outlined a series of work initiatives focused on providing a best-in-class hospitality experience. This plan also transformed Four Seasons' approach to promoting from within. The previously informal approach of the past was replaced with a far more robust system for evaluating potential and performance. The result of this was that the chain was able to find the right people for the right roles.

In other words, it improved the internal process to ensure it delivered a better customer experience.

The glue and the grease represent your organization's purpose and the action it takes. They run in parallel, as one cannot function properly without the other. Having plenty of glue doesn't mean a thing if you don't have a plan for how you will deliver on your purpose. But at the same time, you can't develop a plan without knowing your purpose.

It is in having the grease and glue run parallel to one another that you create collective ambition.

Cost vs. Capability

Let's take a moment to focus on the term "digital transformation." After all, this is what so many organizations aim to create. It is yet another of the supposed "silver bullets" we spoke about earlier that so many organization leaders search for. But like so many silver bullets, digital transformation is not the magical solution to every problem that your organization has.

In fact, I would argue that digital transformation is now a worn, jaded, and watered-down concept! The global pandemic that began in 2020 created a huge shift in the way organizations operate and how customers interact with organizations and has been far more transformative than any internal "Transformation" initiative. Why did it need something so profound and awful to force past organizational inertia?

The result?

We're already in a world where digital comes first. If an organization has failed to adapt to the new digital environment, it's already falling behind those that have and who will be thinking about using the data generated from digital to thrive, perhaps with Machine Learning/Generative and Agentic AI, perhaps with ever more diverse and remote teams, etc. Agile concepts generally come into play in this incrementalism, as they focus on continuous improvements to evolve digital solutions.

In the past, digital solutions, be they software or hardware, came at a huge cost while offering limited capability. As such, the use of digital was restricted to those larger organizations that could afford the technology and actually get something out of it. But as digital has progressed and evolved, we've seen the cost of the solutions and services we use decrease. At the same time, we've seen the capabilities of these solutions increase.

> *Digital costs less than it ever has while offering more than we thought possible a couple of decades ago.*

This reversal of the cost and capability levers means that we need to take a very different approach to managing organizations in the current era. That's what all of this talk about transitioning to agile is really all about. Sticking with the old-world approach to leadership will result in failing to adapt to a rapidly changing organizational environment. As others embrace digital solutions and the enhanced capabilities they provide, you will focus on the costs without recognizing the enormous capability shifts we've seen in recent years.

There needs to be a cultural change in your organization that goes far beyond the original concept of "digital transformation." Creating productive change in your organization is no longer simply about adopting digital solutions. It's about iteration, adaptation, and working out how to use digital to improve internal processes and, by doing so, enhance customer outcomes.

While my Four Easy Steps and many agile methods can be used for more ground-breaking digital transformation, I believe that often organization leaders can kid themselves that respraying IT departments with Agile or framing self-service as innovation will deliver more than useful digital incrementalism. Indeed, the over-hype of tactical success often reduces the ability to have a real compelling vision as victory has already been declared or role-model projects are so trite and banal. The art of real Transformation is to inject "outside-in" innovative ambitious framing of the art of the possible into Step #1—Discovery process.

It's Time to Create Magic

We've covered a lot of this information in this chapter.

You now know about the different levels of competence and knowing, as well as the parallels we can draw between these two issues. We've touched on service design and suggested that designing a service philosophy is the one to follow in the modern era of organization. And finally, we've focused on developing an agile organization that's capable of adapting to the market and evolving technology.

These are all crucial concepts to grasp, as well as fuse, in the world of digital. And hopefully, you can see now that the goal isn't rote "digital transformation." As you're reading this, it's likely your organization has already undergone this supposed era of transformation; at least to some extent. Working with digital in the 21st century is about leaps and then iteration and leaps again. It's about creating an environment where you can uncover your unconscious incompetence, particularly of the outside, lay bare your unknown unknowns, and take action to constantly improve the internal processes and people behaviors in your organization to provide better outcomes for your customers where your people have the confidence to allow change. You won't know where you are trying to head without a North Star or a designed service based on an outside-in view. All of these concepts require you and your people to have the space to think.

And it also helps if you have mixed in a little bit of fairy dust!

In the next chapter, I will introduce the two bits of magic that your organization needs.

CHAPTER FOUR

The Two Bits of Magic—Quality of Ambition and Mixology

W e've all heard of occupational psychology tests for individuals. You know the ones. They're the tests and questionnaires designed to help a person discover their full potential by allowing them to understand the innate qualities that are their keys to success based on benchmarking to other peers who have succeeded in the corporate life of the comparable industry. They are designed to help people identify their development needs, overcome their limitations, lean into their most extraordinary qualities, and ultimately develop a better understanding of who they are and what they bring to the table in the expectation context.

But I want you to imagine that there was a psychology assessment of your organization's real ambition.

Imagine that you ran this assessment in every department of your organization. What would it say? Would it tell you that the goals that each department articulates align with one another? Hopefully, you'd be able to say that your organization's assessment would reveal a cohesive "organizational mind" that's capable of staying focused on realizing its full potential—the sum of the parts. Unfortunately, this often isn't the case. For most organizations, our theoretical assessment would reveal departments with varying ideas on their goals and what quality means in relation to what they're doing. Organizations also often perform these assessments on individuals as if analyzing a wheel nut is all that is required to make the car drive in the right direction.

This, in turn, leads to a muddled mutant vision of the organization's ambition—but it is the one being executed! How can you have a clear, consistent vision when every department and team in your organization has different goals and ideas?

Now, let's imagine that you've run that assessment and received your results, just to assess how worried but hopefully delighted you should be!

Those results outline the psychology of your organization.

If you were to synthesize those results before sitting in a room with your customers or shareholders, what would they say about what you're telling them? Would they agree that your organization's psychology and focus align exactly with their views of what the strategic ambition means to them? Or, would you have a bunch of people wondering just what on earth you're talking about while looking for a buzzword translation app on their mobile device?

Again, it's likely the latter for a lot of organizations.

Now run that experiment again, this time for the hopefully much less troublesome word "quality." The goal here is to check we all agree at least on the quality standard of what is being delivered now. We want to run this little thought experiment to realize that quality is not a static thing that's easily defined. Every department inside your organization may have a different idea of what quality means as it refers to themselves. What's more, your customers and stakeholders may have a completely different view of what quality is to you and your organization. If these definitions of quality and/or vision (ambition) don't align, you end up with an organization that isn't serving its customers.

So, we need to understand what quality means in reference to the people who really matter—those we serve.

What Does Quality Mean?

Quality is massively subjective.

You will discover this if you ever sit down with a group of friends or colleagues to figure out the essential qualities of your product or service. It's doubtful that you will be able to collectively come up with a concrete answer about the quality of the product or service simply because every person in the meeting will have a different idea of what quality means to them. As Harvard University's David Garvin once put it:

> "Quality is an unusually slippery concept, easy to visualize and yet exasperatingly difficult to define."

So many factors can play into a person's definition of a quality product or service. Some focus on the product's performance, while others believe quality comes from a vast array of features. Some may define quality based on the product's reliability or durability. In contrast, others focus more on aesthetics and conformance with what the person expects to gain or experience from the product or service.

Ultimately, quality is subjective and often emotive for the simple fact that everybody approaches the question from their own perspective.

Here, we see one of the key challenges your organization faces. As organization owners, we're often tempted to see our products' qualities through the lens of the properties that are independent of any observation. We focus on solidity, design, patents, and numbers. The goal is to create an unbiased view of quality based on indisputable facts.

However, most of our customers do not perceive quality in the same way. While the cold, hard facts may impress people or convince them to check a product or service out, customers tend to be drawn more to the sensations the product or service creates. Quality for customers often revolves around what they can see, feel, taste, touch, and hear and what emotions are conjured. Defining these sensory experiences is often difficult, leading to the varying perceptions that can often make it challenging to determine what quality actually is. Here, we see something akin to the "I'll know it when I see it" philosophy. While many of us can't put a finger on a perfect definition of quality, we know what it looks and feels like when we find it and then post-rationalize theories as to why we have that feeling.

Mixologists Help Realize Quality of Ambition

How do these concepts about quality relate to your organization?

Let us accept that digital is primarily subjective in its outcomes, with the technology used to achieve quality of ambition. If that is the case, why do we leave so much of our digital strategy in the hands of the logical thinkers inside our companies? Yes, the processes involved in creating and leveraging technology are logical. However, focusing on logic alone means that we miss out on injecting feeling into what we do. As a result, the quality of our ambition ends up being limited by logic because we don't fully understand what our customers and stakeholders hope to feel and experience when using our products.

Think about this in terms of our mixologist metaphor.

You've built an organization designed around running what you are now. That means every process and person you have in place is there to sustain what you are today. Think of these people as your bartenders, who can pour the beer and complete other logical tasks that keep the bar running.

These people are not there to play with the possibilities at hand.

They're not mixologists because they don't live with the ambiguity of potential or aim to get a sense of the customer experience. There is no feeling in pulling a pint of beer. It's a mechanical action that doesn't involve the customer beyond them placing an order for the beer. However, a mixologist takes the time to engage and understand what the customer feels. They enhance an organization's quality of ambition by injecting experiential feeling into the process, thus serving based on the customer's perception of quality rather than our own logical definitions. Your mixologists are creative, insightful, and intuitive. They create a sense of theatre around what you do, focusing on enrapturing your customers with the sights, sounds, and tastes they make. They create value above the sum of the parts.

They're the people who can play with the digital possibilities and mix them into something that's genuinely appealing to customers. And they, along with your organization's quality of ambition, are the two little pieces of magic that we will focus on in this chapter.

You're Living in a VUCA World

Spend enough time around organization consultants and you may eventually hear one of them tell you that we're living in a VUCA world. They're right. However, they're not right in the traditional sense of what VUCA means.

VUCA is an acronym developed by leadership theorists Burt Nanus and Warren Bennis. It was first created to serve as a way for the United States military to describe the ambiguous and potentially unstable world that would result from the end of the Cold War in the late 1980s. The term began to see more frequent usage as we entered the noughties, resulting in many organization leadership experts starting to leverage it as part of their philosophies on strategic leadership.

VUCA stands for the following:

- **Volatility.** This covers the nature and dynamics of change. It also refers to the catalysts that lead to change and the forces that lead to the need for faster change. These catalysts and forces create a world in which we must constantly adapt to changing dynamics.

- **Uncertainty.** Here, we see the lack of predictability in what we do. Think of uncertainty as the potential for surprises to occur that override our understanding of our situation. As uncertainty grows, it becomes harder to make decisions that serve our quality of ambition.

- **Complexity.** We're rarely fortunate enough to only have a single force to contend with at any point in time. Complexity refers to the multitude of forces that confound the issues we're attempting to focus on. These forces create a haziness that makes it challenging to stay focused on what we hope to achieve.

- **Ambiguity.** The mixed meanings we derive from our conditions lead to the potential for misreads and poor decisions. With our realities growing hazier, especially as the other components of VUCA compound, ambiguity grows, leading to an increased likelihood of failure.

To sum it all up, the traditional VUCA model refers to a lot of big and scary stuff. It covers all of the confusion and difficulty we face as organization leaders in defining our quality of ambition and finding a strategic direction to follow. Many experts will tell you that learning about VUCA, and specifically learning about how to mitigate the forces that lead to us living in a VUCA world, is the key to effective management and leadership.

We can see how this model relates to your desire to develop a digital solution that satisfies the market's needs. You're watching that market change constantly, alongside the technology that you can use to create your solution. For you, VUCA may refer to having so many options available, with new ones being added all the time, that you end up too overwhelmed to create a concrete direction for your organization. You may, of course, not be watching the outside world and market at all and be ignorantly happy, which is a different problem.

While I can see the relevance, I have a problem with the traditional VUCA model. I agree that it's essential to understand the components of the Nanus and Bennis model. But I don't feel that VUCA is the be-all and end-all of awareness and readiness that many make it out to be, at least not in its current form. I recognize that it represents the feelings that many have about working in a more fluid world where taking the next steps forward seems complicated because of the level of uncertainty in the air. However, I also feel that this traditional VUCA model engenders fear of so many possibilities to the point where it can limit your ability to set a strategic direction, rather than enhance it. The other symptom of a general inability to handle ambiguity and complexity is the herd effect around hyped technology: Cloud, AI, Agentic, etc. As much as you may feel that you're living in this version of a VUCA world, and you're far from alone in those feelings, I believe that VUCA means something different from the above for today's leaders. VUCA needs to evolve for the digital era, and it lacks constraints and endless possibilities.

The New VUCA World

Perhaps my biggest issue with the traditional VUCA model is that it focuses entirely on the problems without hinting at how to read the runes, prioritize, or sense the solutions to those problems. We can all read the definitions provided in the model, nod along, and agree that we're living in a VUCA world and "someone" should do something about it. But suppose that's where our understanding of VUCA ends. In that case, we're left in a fearful state in which we achieve nothing because we don't know how to confront all of the instability that we often feel we face when attempting to implement digital solutions or introduce new products and services to the market.

So, how about we flip the script?

How about we create a VUCA model that focuses on achieving your quality of ambition rather than one that's all about how crappy and uncertain the world can feel? In this model, we'll come up with some new definitions for each of the letters in the acronym. Each of these new definitions acts as a direct counter to the issues the traditional model highlights, starting with:

Vision

When volatility occurs, we can meet and overcome it through the strength of our vision. Through this vision, we commit to accepting and embracing change rather than treating it as some sort of scary bogeyman that we need to run away from or somehow learn to live with.

Start by creating a clear statement of the values your organization holds. Building from those values, create a shared future vision that defines what your team should aim to achieve. Think of this in the context of the various definitions of quality that each department in the organization can come up with. By developing a defined vision, we get rid of this disparity and create a universal statement of quality that all departments align with.

Understanding

The best way to counter uncertainty is to develop understanding. This means taking time to pause and examine your market and the organization's environment. What is it telling you? What can you learn from listening to your customers? What is their definition of quality, and how can you ensure you deliver it to them?

Understanding is all about staying on top of what's happening in your industry. That goes beyond listening to your customers. You must also leverage competitive intelligence and pay attention to target market news. The more you know about what's happening in your market, the clearer your understanding of your customers' needs.

Clarity

Increased clarity causes complexity to melt away. And the best way to create clarity is to focus on communication, both inside your organization and in terms of how you communicate with customers.

Internally, the focus lies on creating clear communication channels that allow you to express the goals and needs of the organization without any confusion. Focus on developing a collaborative work environment where your people feel free to add their ideas into the mix. It's these ideas that your mixologists will pick up and start building on when developing solutions for your customers.

Speaking of customers, understand that communication is a two-way street. By listening to your customers, rather than attempting to dictate to them, you develop a better understanding of what they want and what they perceive quality to be.

Adaptability

'The best-laid plans of mice and men' will crumble into the dust when ambiguity muddies the water. That means the plans we create have to be adaptable to the environment we find ourselves in. In developing a flexible, agile, and adaptable culture, we can overcome ambiguity by pivoting to suit the situation.

Your people are the key here.

Hire people who thrive and build confidence in others when confronted with the challenges that a VUCA world presents. Build an ideas culture that empowers your people to share their thoughts. Reward those who align with the qualities the new VUCA model embraces and, perhaps most importantly, be the leader who encourages adaptability in the workplace. Instead of relying on what has always worked in the past, understand that a VUCA world requires flexible, adaptable leadership capable of combating ambiguity with agility and ideation. Yes, we live in a VUCA world. However, VUCA is much more than one of those annoying organization buzzwords that we all nod along to without getting anything actionable out of it.

The new model of VUCA offers us the counterpoints to all of the problems that the traditional model presents.

It allows us to create clarity and flexibility while empowering us to discover a quality of ambition that aligns with our customers' perceptions of quality. Through the new VUCA, you also equip your (own or rented, full-time or fractional, etc.) mixologists with all of the tools and incentives they need because you create a collaborative organization in which ideas are constantly added to a melting pot, just waiting for your mixologists to create something that feels amazing out of them.

VUCA is not something for us to fear. We must all aspire to follow this model when building a flexible and dynamic digital organization.

Creating Flow in Your Organization

We have all heard of the idea of being "in the flow." It is far from a new concept. However, flow is one of those interesting ideas wherein it's easy to know when you're in flow, but creating the right environment to enter flow is less easily understood. In that way, we can perhaps draw a parallel between flow and quality. You know it when you have it, but everything leading up to it can feel shrouded in confusion.

Do you instinctively believe that the momentum from Flow is more cost-effective and sustainable than Transformation specialists doing things to you?

Still, flow is an essential part of achieving consistent quality. And to create that quality, you must first answer this critical question about your quality of ambition:

Why are you bothering at all, and what will make your digital solution competitively different?

It sounds like a harsh question. However, the point of asking is to establish why you want to create a digital transformation in the first place. It's to establish a purpose beyond the fact that everybody else seems to be doing it. Without your own purpose in place, your own reason for why you're bothering to do this, pushing for any sort of change in your organization will almost inevitably lead to failure or a "cut 'n' paste" job. You'll see the effort as more of an annoyance than something you're fully engaged in. As a result, your lack of quality of ambition will lead to a lack of quality in your product or service.

These ideas relating to purpose bring us back to flow.

In their paper, *The Theory of "Flow" and its Relevance for Organizations Part: 1*, Zoltán Buzády and Paul Marer provide us with their definition of flow:

> *"Another label for Flow is 'peak experience' or 'being in a Zone'. Flow experiences have limited duration, ranging from a few minutes to several hours; never more than a working day. One can periodically re-enter a Flow state -- in ideal situations, at increasingly higher combinations of challenges and skills."*

They also draw a parallel between the concepts of flow and engagement. The only difference between the two, they contend, is that flow is a temporary state that can occur, while engagement is more prolonged and potentially permanent. I bring this up because purpose is a precondition of engagement. When your people feel like they have no meaningful purpose, they will not feel engaged with their task and consequently have little pride and accountability. In this case, lacking a reason why you want to achieve digital transformation will lead to the sort of people resistance we spoke about in earlier chapters. Your quality of ambition will not show your people why they should bother, so, to put it bluntly, they won't. A lack of engagement will exist, resulting in lower-quality output.

I bring this up because the same paper also highlights the eight preconditions of entering the flow state. We want to meet these preconditions because they place us and our people in a state where we perform at our highest level. The preconditions are as follows:

1. A balance between skills and challenges
2. Clear goals
3. Clear, immediate, and constructive feedback
4. Effortless action
5. Intense concentration
6. Sense of control
7. Lack of awareness of time passing
8. Doing an activity because it feels good rather than doing it for any external reward.

While each of the eight is important, it's numbers 1 and 8 that I want you to focus on. With the eighth precondition, we see that the activity a person is doing must feel good to them. Again, this is where our sense of purpose and our quality of ambition come in. If you don't care about what you're doing because there is no purpose behind it, you won't feel good about the task. It will hinder you, drain your time, and prevent you from doing what you actually want to do. As such, you will not enter the flow state, meaning you will not achieve the level of quality that you hope to achieve. I do believe that eight needs to be aligned to the useful purpose.

The balance between challenge and skill is another necessary condition. One of the most significant issues related to achieving digital transformation is that the challenge you face can feel overwhelming (and perhaps if it doesn't, you are spending too much effort delivering a commodity). With so many options and such a rapidly changing environment, the scale of that challenge may not match up to your current skill level. As such, you will not achieve flow because you constantly have to stop and start your work to learn more or try to improve your skill levels.

So, to create flow in our organizations, we must focus on the eight preconditions that Buzády and Marer highlight, with a particular focus on the level of challenge and the purpose behind what we're doing. In achieving flow, you enter a state where you can play at the top of your game. Ideas flow freely and you can realize your true quality of ambition.

Flow also plays into the mixology concept. If we see mixologists as weavers of the art of possibilities under the constraints of the reality of their capabilities, we again see how the alignment between challenge and skill comes into play. If the challenge is too high, our mixologists cannot perform at their peak. The organization can't build momentum because everything it does has a stop-start feel.

Ultimately, the goal is to create a working environment that enables entering the flow state. Doing this makes it more likely that we achieve the digital outcomes we want. You have the eight preconditions that Buzády and Marer highlighted in their paper. Now, let's look at six steps that build from these preconditions, allowing you to create a culture where flow is more likely to occur.

Step #1—Focus on Satisfaction Over Profits

[Note: if you are a not-for-profit organization, please substitute your North Star measures.]

In the modern business world, profit is king or queen. It is the cornerstone of an organization that we all must chase to both sustain our companies and satisfy our shareholders. The latter group (in the for-profit sector), in particular, tends to care about little else but the profit. They've invested in you and if they don't see returns on that investment, they disappear. Our shareholders want to see a profit and, frankly, many often don't care precisely or prescriptively how that profit is achieved. They're not looking for you to build a sustainable organization or achieve any sort of transformation. They, as long as the profits continue somehow, want to see good numbers in the profit and loss statement and little else.

This isn't necessarily a terrible thing. A focus on profit is crucial to the success of any organization. However, focusing solely on profit, to the point where it becomes the priority for the organization, can result in the micromanagement of our efforts— "penny wise and pound foolish." We measure outputs and track key performance indicators, getting so lost in the numbers that we lose focus on what's actually happening inside our organizations in relation to future viability.

In doing so, we also lose focus on one of our critical preconditions of flow—doing an activity because it feels good without needing material rewards.

So many of the solutions organizations use to increase profitability focus on incentivizing the workforce through material rewards. We offer commissions for sales, bonuses for high levels of performance, and other little rewards that make it clear to our people that their work is valued based on their profit or drivers of profit, such as Sales output. Again, I'm not saying that these forms of incentivization don't have their place. But if you combine them with a workforce that does not feel as though there is any sort of quality of ambition behind what they're doing, you create a recipe for detachment or burnout, paint by numbers, soulless obedience or organizational introversion instead of flow.

To counter this, we must strive for happiness in our organizations. True happiness comes from feeling satisfied in life because we have the opportunity to reach our true potential with our colleagues.

When people are happy, their employers receive the best of them. Why is this not often seen as a mission or goal for a business?

They're more engaged in their work, which means they're also more likely to enter the flow state, which results in higher levels of productivity and creativity.

Step #2—Create an Environment Where Happiness and Profit Meet

Mihaly Csikszentmihalyi, a psychologist we can think of as the father of research into the flow state, tells us that profit and happiness do not have to be disparate concepts. You can have both if you create the right conditions. In fact, the pursuit of profit can play into increasing the happiness levels of your team. As Csikszentmihalyi tells us, for somebody to feel happy in their work, they must have the desire to do great work while also feeling like what they do contributes to something larger than themselves.

Enabling digital transformation, thus creating an organization that's able to generate more profit, is larger than any single individual in an organization.

So, if our first step focused on how you should no longer make profit your sole priority, our next step is all about making sure you don't lose sight of profit entirely. Without profit, an organization cannot be successful. It won't be able to sustain itself. It certainly won't be able to grow as there will be no money in the [digital] wallet to fund that growth. In these situations, people stop feeling like they're working towards something bigger than themselves and instead begin to feel like they're 'flogging a dead horse. They can see that the purpose behind the organization is going unfulfilled because the money isn't there to follow that purpose.

In this sense, we can see happiness and profit as being two sides of the same coin. Without happiness, our people can't enter the state of flow, so they don't reach the levels of performance required for high profits. And without profit, happiness is not sustainable because we lose our ability to meet our quality of ambition, regardless of how clear that quality is. So, we must create working environments in which respect for both conditions exists if we hope to achieve flow regularly.

If you have not thought of creating a healthy flow in your organization, you may see symptoms such as friction between functions, quality issues, customer complaints, and morale issues.

Step #3—Allow for Deep Work to Occur

Georgetown University professor Cal Newport came up with the concept of deep work. Conveniently, he also described it for us:

"Deep Work: Professional activities performed in a state of distraction-free concentration that pushes your cognitive capabilities to their limit. These efforts create new value, improve your skill, and are hard to replicate."

We can immediately see how this relates to several of the preconditions of flow that Buzády and Marer outlined. For deep work to occur, somebody must have an intense concentration on work that pushes their skills to the limit without the challenge being so enormous that it exceeds their cognitive capabilities.

We can boil this down to creating an environment where our people are not constantly distracted by other tasks. Every ring of the phone, ping of an email notification, and non-productive meeting a person attends is a distraction that prevents entry into the flow state. This idea that people must be capable of multitasking is a misnomer for the simple fact that multitasking prevents focus on quality outcomes for a single task. So, to enable flow, you must offer distraction-free workplaces while encouraging a single-task mentality. This does not mean only assigning a single task to your people. Instead, it's about encouraging them to focus on one task at a time, giving it their full attention so they can achieve the intense concentration levels required for flow. Variety in work is stimulating, but thrashing between different tasks is inefficient and unproductive.

If you have not thought about allowing for deep work, then you may see symptoms such as complaining noise about too many meetings, lots of test defects, and designs that are 'meh.

Step #4—Create Clarity in Your Organization

It's here where we see our most apparent link between flow and our ideas about the quality of ambition and purpose. Flow can only occur when your people understand the meaning behind what they're doing. That purpose has to be crystal clear, with no room for ifs, ands, or buts. In the case of digital transformation (see note above about transition v transformation), it's not enough to say that your organization needs to go digital. You also need to be able to explain why the change must occur and how it serves the people responsible for creating it if you want them to do more than go through the motions.

Creating clarity is all about connecting the dots inside your organization.

As a leader, it's our job to show your people how Point A links to Point B, which connects to Point C, and so on. In other words, we must help our people understand how whatever tasks they're doing now, no matter how small, contribute to the organization's broader purpose. This clarity helps to create the link between happiness and meaning, which Csikszentmihalyi highlights as an essential component of the flow state.

Step #5—Support Autonomy

What does a digital mixologist need to succeed inside your organization?

They need the space to be creative so they can mesh ideas together. A mixologist must understand what your customers want and should be able to work with limited constraints.

Perhaps most of all, they need a level of autonomy to create the right momentum.

Setting performance targets and other success measures that focus purely on profit limits a person's ability to think creatively. Our people can become slaves to the target, working in service of it, with the target becoming a critical focus that distracts away from the actual task. As a leader, your mission is to strike a balance between hitting targets and creating the autonomy a mixologist needs to enter the flow state.

This is tricky.

The goal here is to allow our people to figure out the "how" themselves, with minimal interference from management. Your role is to assess the outcome and provide the feedback needed to allow your mixologist to build on what they're doing until they come up with the perfect cocktail for your customers. Offer clear and constructive feedback without going so overboard that you take control of the task and hamper your mixologists in their efforts.

Step #6—Encourage Growth

With this final step, we come back to the precondition of finding a balance between skill and challenge. When a task is so simplistic that you feel like you can do it in your sleep, flow is unattainable because you'll never be engaged in the task. That lack of engagement means you can't achieve the high levels of concentration needed for flow. You can't get lost in the task because the task itself does not challenge you.

Conversely, a task that is so challenging that it overwhelms your skill level makes you feel like you're not capable of achieving anything. That serves to demotivate just as powerfully as a task that requires no effort.

So, our goal here is to find that balance between skill and challenge. In doing so, we encourage growth by pushing our people, and especially our mixologists, to the limits of their capabilities. Upon reaching this limit, our people develop their skills, enabling them to take on more challenging tasks in the future.

Ultimately, this final step is all about understanding the skill-based constraints your people have so you ensure everything you ask of them fits right at the edges of those constraints. Empower your people by encouraging them to learn and engage with the task, creating the growth that is so essential for the realization of your ambitions.

The Defense Mechanisms That Hamper Ambition

So, we have established that quality of ambition, combined with mixologists who are in flow, are the two bits of magic that enable digital transformation. However, there is a challenge inherent in having a high quality of ambition. Even when your people understand the purpose behind the change you're trying to create, they may still rebel against it. We touched on this in Chapter Three when discussing the concept of inertia. No matter how clear the need for transformation may be, some people may meet change with a lack of desire or risk aversion and, in some cases, resistance.

Why does this happen?

Change resistance is a natural tendency for most people. They need time to receive, process, and interpret information using the lenses of their values and lived experiences.

Additionally and on top, change resistance often occurs because a person has had or heard of a bad experience with change at some point in their lives. This lousy experience creates the mindset that change is something to avoid, leading to the mind creating what psychologists call "defense mechanisms" to protect against even potential change or risk in the future.

We can look at defense mechanisms as ways that a person thinks or acts that prevent them from engaging in an activity that their minds are trying to protect them from. If that activity is changed, then your organization has a severe problem. Change-related defense mechanisms hamper your quality of ambition because they create barriers you must overcome before you can realize that ambition. Your mixologists become less effective because they constantly have to combat these defenses. Ultimately, you end up with an organization with no flow, leading to you getting sluggish and stuck as the world moves on. People move through their change curves at different speeds and interact with each other in positive or negative ways, making organizational change complex and difficult to manage well. [If you have not heard of Change Curves, please take a look: https://www.ekrfoundation.org/5-stages-of-grief/change-curve/]

So, what can we do about these defense mechanisms?

Our first task is to identify what they are. By knowing what we're dealing with, we can start taking steps to lower the defense, allowing for a more change-oriented mindset. With that in mind, let's highlight some of the key defense mechanisms you may encounter, which may or may not be easily visible when trying to create digital change.

Mechanism #1—Denial

Perhaps the most common defense mechanism, denial, is the refusal to accept the facts of a situation and can have many causes from inside-out inertia, fear, confusion, insulation from the market through to being too comfortable and disinclination to change.

We see this all the time when trying to foster digital transformation. Our people can see that the reality is that the organization will get overtaken by other forces if it is not agile enough to adapt to the current situation. And yet, the pervading opinion may still be that we can continue doing what we're already doing without worrying about the changing reality around us. Of course, the inevitable happens, and the organization stagnates. By blocking out reality, that reality ends up overwhelming us.

In many cases, a sharp dose of reality is the key to overcoming this mechanism. By making the facts as clear as day, to the point where they're undeniable, a person can be helped to avoid denial. They should accept what is right in front of them because this mechanism often crumbles when confronted with facts it cannot deny (people can and do still deny the facts and get stuck in this phase). There is also a longer-term cultural approach around perceptions of safety in change and elimination of blame cultures to foster a "why not?" mindset over time.

Mechanism #2—Regression

Let's say that you've begun the implementation process for your digital transformation. New software packages are installed, you have training in place for your people, and the transition from the old to the new is underway.

However, some of your people aren't taking to the new systems. In fact, they're actively refusing to use them properly, instead favoring the previous systems you had in place.

That is a regression in action. Regression is a concerted move back to an earlier stage in development. For example, an adult who feels stressed out and overwhelmed may regress to a more childlike state, in which they avoid responsibilities in favor of activities that don't require them to think about the situation. In an organizational context, we see regression when people go back to working in a way that was comfortable to them in the past, leading to outright rejection of the new way of working that you're trying to implement. Of course, this repression hampers ambition because it creates a schism in the organization, with some adopting the new way while others fall back on the old. This lack of alignment makes it impossible to create a culture of mixology because you face a constant battle to try and keep the two sides aligned. This seems an apt time to recommend more on Flow by considering the Water Logic works of Edward de Bono.

> *"Most disagreements are really based on differences of context. Yet we usually direct our thinking to arguing about differences of 'truth'." Edward de Bono*

Mechanism #3—Rationalization

If people can find the logic behind their behavior, they can rationalize what they're doing. We can think of this as a defense mechanism that protects the ego. We do something wrong, so we find a way to justify the action.

This commonly crops up as a culture of blame in organizations. The sales team rationalizes that they can't attract new clients because the marketing team isn't doing a good enough job of supplying qualified leads. Our marketers may rationalize not being able to find leads because they don't have the budget or the product isn't interesting enough to consumers.

In the case of digital transformation, rationalizations tend to form around the idea that a person can do what they need to do without the aid of digital technology. As such, they should be left to do the job they want to. After all, it's getting done, right?

The problem with rationalization is that it eventually devolves into excuses for why a person should (or should not) do something. For example, somebody may still be able to rationalize not adapting to digital because other people in the organization can do it. They don't need to adapt because others can do it for them. Of course, this fails to account for the fact that organization-wide adaptation leads to far greater outcomes.

Mechanism #4—Projection

Projection occurs when we try to place our own feelings and thoughts into the minds of others. For example, you may have a co-worker that you dislike, perhaps for reasons that you don't truly understand. Instead of accepting this dislike for what it is, enabling you to work around it, you project your feelings onto the co-worker. You reason that you must dislike this person because they dislike you. It doesn't matter if you have any evidence to support this conclusion. Reaching the conclusion is evidence in itself, with anything that the co-worker may then do serving to build on the conclusion. You end up seeing what you want to see in their actions, even when said actions are completely innocuous.

Of course, projection can occur in the context of digital transformation when people assume that others have the same distaste for the transformation as they do. In projecting their feelings onto others, those who hamper ambition provide themselves with a good enough reason to continue their behavior.

Mechanism #5—Displacement

This mechanism is the redirection of the feelings and thoughts you may have for one person onto another.

Of course, we have the classic example of the irate employee who hates their boss to lean on here. The employee feels like they can't express their feelings to the boss, leading to them bottling those feelings up. However, those feelings need to go somewhere.

Perhaps said employee goes home and screams at their partner. Or, they get into an argument with a co-worker, releasing their frustration at the boss in the process.

This defense mechanism protects the person from potentially angering whoever is the source of their ire. However, it does so by creating fractures in other relationships that actually have nothing to do with the anger the person feels. Typically, this defense mechanism takes root when employees feel like they're unable to openly communicate with their managers. As such, creating an environment in which feedback, both positive and constructively negative, is encouraged can go a long way to ensuring this defense mechanism doesn't hamper your ambition.

Mechanism #6—Avoidance

Another of the most common defense mechanisms, avoidance, is also the simplest. When faced with a challenge that we don't want to meet, we avoid doing it as much as we can. In an organizational context, this usually shows up as procrastination. The employee who tells you that they'll complete their training another day is avoiding the training, for example.

Thankfully, this may also be the easiest defense mechanism to confront. You can tell almost instantly if someone avoids a task because their productivity declines. They'll give you a bunch of reasons why they can't do something right now, though those reasons are often simple to see through.

Still, that doesn't make avoidance any less effective as a means of hampering your quality of ambition. If your people are avoiding digital transformation, be it through failure to implement or even refusal to talk about the idea of creating transformation, you have a challenge to overcome. In this case, clear communication that confronts the avoidance can often help to break the pattern, allowing you to realize your digital outcomes.

Mechanism #7—Reaction Formation

From one of the simpler mechanisms, we move into something more complex. With reaction formation, people recognize that they have certain feelings about a subject. However, they counter those feelings by trying to force a reaction that is the opposite of what their instincts are telling them. For example, let's say that one of your people feels wary about digital transformation. They feel the purpose behind it hasn't been explained coherently enough. This means they don't understand the ambition behind it or how they can contribute to the culture of mixology you're trying to create. In short, there's a lot of negativity about the transformation bubbling up inside. Instead of expressing their feelings, somebody with this defense mechanism will express complete positivity. They'll agree with everything being said and act like somebody completely on board with the transformation.

However, this reaction is not authentic. The frustrations and feelings the person has aren't confronted properly, leading to them struggling during the transformation. Without knowing it, this person may hamper ambition because they feel unable to express their true feelings about the project. A lack of expression leads to poor communication, resulting in the breakdown of the relationship between employee and manager. So again, the possible remedy to this defense mechanism is to encourage feedback in your organization, ensuring your people feel comfortable with expressing their wariness as well as their support for the transformation.

Mechanism #8—Aggressiveness

There is a fine line to tread between assertiveness and aggressiveness when putting an opinion across.

Being assertive means conveying your opinions firmly and directly while ensuring you show respect to the person you're speaking to. Assertiveness shows confidence in your opinion, meaning it's something that we should aim for.

Unfortunately, assertiveness can transform into aggression when a person is incapable of believing that any opinion other than their own can possibly be right. Aggressive people are less capable of listening with empathy, meaning that they don't understand the needs and ideas of others. They often pay lip service to listening before countering any points they disagree with by shouting them down.

This is a defense mechanism that some managers employ when they feel as though somebody is questioning their authority.

Naturally, this runs counter to the entire concept of mixology, which requires constant feedback and the challenging of existing ideas. Aggressiveness hampers ambition because it leads to silencing ideas that could lead to the fulfillment of ambition. Passive aggression is the silent killer of progress.

Mechanism #9—Undoing

Imagine that you're in a meeting with a group of your people. You're all discussing digital transformation and appear to be on the same page regarding your approach. Suddenly, somebody pipes up with an opinion that runs counter to the meeting's general tone. This isn't necessarily a problem for you, as you want your people to feel comfortable expressing their true opinions and this type of feedback will help create a smoother implementation.

However, it appears to be a problem for the person who expressed their opinion.

In the hours following the meeting, this person may speak to you about their opinion. Rather than explaining their reasoning, they try to take it back by praising the plan excessively. This is the defense mechanism of undoing in action. It occurs when we feel so guilty about an expressed opinion or thought that we do everything we can to undo it so we can act like it never happened. Sometimes, the person may claim that they are representing the "team", which can be a cultural concern if it is true.

This is a problem because it creates an unclear picture of a person's true opinion. Undoing makes it difficult to implement change because you can never quite feel sure that everybody is on board with the plan. Again, the key to overcoming this defense mechanism is to encourage all forms of communication, with a particular emphasis on allowing people to express their misgivings. Encourage your people to dig deeper into their reasons for having an opposing opinion instead of trying to convince them about the correctness of your opinion. In doing so, you may uncover some legitimate issues.

The Keys to Mixology

What do we need to allow digital mixology to occur in our organizations?

Quality of ambition (and its consistent comprehension) is the first, and perhaps most important, key. If you cannot define a purpose for the change you hope to create, you're very unlikely to convince others that the change is needed in the first place. They'll see no reason to bother with the change, leading to an organization that stagnates as the environment changes around it.

Redefining what it means to live in a VUCA world is another key. You switch your culture from fearing the uncertainty and ambiguity of the modern organization world to being capable of adapting to it. The new VUCA model presented in this chapter allows you to create clarity while removing uncertainty, allowing your people to feel more comfortable with the ideas that your mixologists present.

Finally, we have the concept of flow. Encouraging flow is crucial because it's when you are in the flow state that your people can work to their full potential. However, flow cannot occur when the conditions for it do not exist. We've covered those conditions extensively, so I won't reiterate them here. What I will say is that your quality of ambition plays directly into the ability to create the flow that allows your mixologists to thrive. A lack of purpose behind your ambition makes it difficult for people to engage with digital transformation. By providing purpose, we have one of the vital components for making flow possible. From there, it's a case of ensuring the working environment allows for flow.

However, the environment alone is not enough to create an organization that flows. As we've seen in this chapter, along with previous ones, your people are also crucial. When your people throw up defense mechanisms in response to your efforts to create change, you end up with an organization in inertia. In this chapter, we've covered some of the possible defense mechanisms you may encounter. We've also discussed how perceptions of quality vary depending on who you're talking to.

Edward de Bono defined the formula:

Flow + Change > Resistance =
Digital Momentum

Change costs are usually premium costs, so flow is a continuous and more cost-effective approach. However, this means that you need to take a humanist view rather than a mechanical view of the context for your digital.

The mind can only see what it is prepared to see. Therefore, the loops and paradigms that cause resistance to digitization must be understood and acceptable alternatives made to feel safe. To extrapolate to an organizational level, think of yourself in terms of "Rock Logic" and "Water Logic" (using the thinking from Edward de Bono's Water Logic book) and then multiply based on the number of people in your organization.

"Rock Logic" focuses on rigid, fixed truths, while "Water Logic" emphasizes adaptability and the importance of context.

Here's a breakdown of the key differences:

Rock Logic

- **Focus**: Fixed, absolute truths and facts.
- **Approach**: Rigid, unyielding, and resistant to change.
- **Example**: "This is the only way to do it" or "This is always true."
- **Thinking Style**: Linear and logical, often prioritizing accuracy and precision.

Water Logic

- **Focus**: Context, flow, and adaptability.

- **Approach**: Flexible, fluid, and open to change.
- **Example**: "This is true in this context, but might change in another," or "Let's see how things flow."
- **Thinking Style**: Lateral and creative, often valuing exploration and understanding.

In essence, Rock Logic is about finding the right answer, while Water Logic is about understanding the situation and the flow of possibilities. Rock Logic can be useful for tasks requiring precision and accuracy, while Water Logic is helpful for complex situations where flexibility and adaptability are needed.

Water Logic emphasizes that "truth" is often context-dependent, while Rock Logic tends to view truth as absolute and unchanging.

If you add more water to water, the new water becomes part of the whole. If you add a rock to a rock, you simply have two rocks.
Edward de Bono.

These quotes from Edward de Bono are particularly pertinent to the current SaaS era, which is replacing previous bespoke data prisons with a vendor model where the vendor controls your access to your data, an extreme inside-out mindset.

In the next chapter, we examine how people, both your customers and colleagues, are your true power and can add to your flow (i.e., market momentum).

CHAPTER FIVE

Your People Are Your Power

And so, we return home to our cocktail bar metaphor.

If you believe that people are just something we have not automated to unemployment yet with technology, then this should be an interesting chapter if you can suspend judgment for a moment.

By now, you understand that your mixologist can greatly impact your organization. In the last chapter, we established how these are the people who can help you figure out what your customer's definition of quality is and how they can move you forward in the context of market ambiguity that can lead you to otherwise copy competitors. Your mixologists take the outside-in approach, becoming completely immersed in how their customers think, empowering them to serve the customer's qualitative and quantitative needs.

However, your mixologist can only do so much when hampered by a lack of organizational goals. As we learned in the previous chapter, a lack of quality of ambition means your mixologist cannot fully connect or engage with your customers—the mandate is hampered, and the frame is too zoomed. To use the full powers of a mixologist, you've got to focus on your people and culture to unlock potential.

How an organization approaches people and culture has a material effect on the digital mixologist's chances of success. It also affects your chances of building a sustainable and growing organization where digital seeps deeper into it.

In other words,

It's up to you to create an environment where your mixologist can succeed and your organization thrives.

We can quickly see how this applies in the cocktail bar. The décor and design of the bar help to set the mood that the mixologist aims to enhance. Ensuring the mixologist has all of the ingredients they need to create the cocktails that their customers want is also critical. If you're missing some vital ingredients, you tie your mixologist's hands, forcing them to serve up their best facsimile of what the customer wants, even though they know it's not completely right. As the bar owner, your goal is to create the vibe that patrons want to keep returning to.

Your focus should be an environment that empowers your mixologist to do great things for the bar.

If we shift this metaphor to the traditional organization setting, your digital mixologist isn't going to need great décor and appropriate mood music to set the stage for them to display their talents. Instead, they will need the technological tools that enable the digital transformation you hope to create. But perhaps most importantly, they need you to realize one crucial thing when it comes to digital.

Your people are your power. They know what good, great, or exceptional looks like when it comes to their personal lives—get them to bring those standards to work rather than be passengers to corporate meh! In the Dedication I asked whether you would enjoy the taste of your digital if it were a cocktail. What would your people say if asked the same question? This goes for both the people inside your organization and those you serve with your products and services.

In understanding the role that people play in mixology and digital transformation, we can create the appropriate environment for our mixologists to showcase their skills.

It's Not Hard

It's not hard to leverage the power of your people to help your mixologist create digital change.

That may seem like a harsh point, especially to somebody who's found themselves struggling to adapt to digital. However, the point stands that it should be extremely easy to walk in your customers' shoes so you can understand their experiences and their points of view.

A long, long time ago, I wanted to buy a telephone answering machine. I wanted one that would start recording after six to eight rings to give me a chance to find and get to the phone. But do you think I could find a single website anywhere that sold the exact type of answering machine I wanted? I couldn't find a single website on the planet for something as fundamental as an answering machine that told me how many rings the machine allowed before it clicked in and started recording.

Doesn't that seem like valuable information to you?

If you own an answering machine, you want to know that it gives you some leeway for answering a call before it clicks into action. Knowing how much leeway helps me make a decision. I don't want a machine that clicks in after two rings because that means I've got to make a mad dash to the phone to answer it before it starts recording. At the same time, I don't want a machine that takes a dozen rings because most callers aren't going to wait that long before hanging up.

Between six and eight was perfect for me. Yet, I couldn't find a website that gave me this seemingly basic information.

Now, there are two lessons we can take from this little story (other than that I am aging, and 50% of you probably have no clue what a landline or answering machine is!).

The first is that every organization that sells answering machines appears too lazy to type out the information I wanted to find or too inside-out to think of features from a customer point of view. However, I don't think that's the case. The products I found had plenty of other information. They were all just missing this fundamental thing that would help me to make my purchasing decision.

The second lesson comes when you see what happened when I eventually bought my answering machine. I ended up being forced to make a decision without the information that I wanted. And wouldn't you just know it, I ended up with an answering machine that always clicked on after two rings (please don't laugh!).

Of course, that answering machine ended up going back to the supplier. But I share this story to show that there are still so many issues with how companies market their products to customers. In this case, we see a sin of omission, with no retailer on the planet seeming to think that the customer might want to know how many rings they get before they have to answer the phone. If just one of these companies placed themselves in their customers' shoes, they'd realize that this is actually a pretty crucial piece of information. I'm far from the only person who wants to know how many rings an answering machine gives me. It's a logical thing to want to know. I did eventually get one with a long ring cycle in the end through random luck—but sadly, I discovered that if there was an old message, then it dropped from six to two rings as an apparently beneficial feature—I guess it would be for burglars to know who was out.

More importantly, it's a question that has a really easy answer.

I have another example.

I'm based in the UK and get my energy from British Gas. Recently, they sent me an email telling me that I needed to arrange a service for my boiler. Okay, that sounds fine. What do I do next?

That email wasn't about to tell me. It didn't provide me with my username, so I had to trawl through my records to figure out what username I'd used to sign up for their website in the first place. Worse yet, the email didn't give me a link to the page I needed to go to so I could set up an appointment. I had to find the link myself without help from the organization. And when I found that link, it told me that I couldn't arrange a servicing appointment right now as they were busy.

Why then send me the email?

It's not hard to see that British Gas shouldn't have bothered sending me such a useless email. It's also not hard to see the various failings in customer service with both of these examples. That is my point. So many organizations focus on serving their customers through the lens of their own organizational structures, low-level measures, and dysfunctionality through lack of flow. That's what causes the sins of omission and the pointless emails that so many of these companies send out.

Companies seem to spend a lot of energy not doing the simple things right for the customer.

Why is that?

They don't understand that the people they serve are their true value and power or they know you are trapped with them.

Customer Engagement Pays Off

I'm going to hit you with a few stats about customer engagement.

According to CRM organization SuperOffice, if you're capable of offering a great customer experience, 86% of people are willing to pay more for your service than they'd pay an organization that offers a poor experience.

Customer insight platform Lumoa highlights that 39% of companies fail to elicit feedback from their customers about the interactions these customers have with the organization regularly.

Common sense, right? But here's the most important one:

Gallup tells us that Business to Business (B2B) companies that successfully engage their customers achieve 55% higher profits,

63% lower customer attrition, and 50% higher productivity. We've just spent an entire chapter examining the concept of flow, which directly relates to the productivity of your people through continuous momentum and progress rather than stop-start disruption. Here, we see how the critical element of customer engagement leads to much higher productivity and performance in our organizations.

And yet, as we see from my earlier stories, too many companies overlook the importance of engaging their customers. They omit key information or bombard customers with useless emails that don't tell them what they need to do. Every little faux pas serves to disengage customers. When an organization has disengaged customers, it almost inevitably ends up with letting the competition in and disengaged and unmotivated workers who may underperform, quietly quit, or jump ship.

So, the obvious message to take from this is that we need to work harder to engage our customers. The obvious question from this message is, "What can we do to keep our customers engaged?"

The answer lies in a concept that we introduced earlier in the book.

Being agile enough to adapt to changing customer expectations is the key to keeping them engaged. For example, 87% of UK adults use a smartphone, with 60% having two devices they use regularly. This means most customers have easier access to the organizations from which they buy than ever before. They can jump online to find a phone number to call. They can head to a website to send a message via a contact form or through email. If they're lucky, they may even be able to engage in a live chat via an organization's website to discuss their issues.

…If they're lucky.

Despite knowing that customers have the tools to engage with us so readily, we often provide them with few ways to stay engaged. Instead, organizations bombard customers with emails that aren't relevant, don't serve any personal needs, and at a frequency that makes no sense to most recipients. So many companies treat their customers as though they're just numbers, failing to engage them on a personal level even though digital offers all of the tools they'll ever need to do just that. Companies just aren't taking advantage of what they have to better understand their customers so they can align what they do best with what their customers want.

Inevitably, these organizations fail to reap the benefits of customer engagement because they're not actively trying to keep customers engaged and listened to.

The critical point I want to make here is that customer engagement pays off. We can see that from the stats I shared earlier. Engaged customers spend more money and stick with the companies that serve them. Most importantly, having engaged customers motivates our people to do more for those customers. When I talk about creating the ideal environment for your mixologists to work in, this is what I'm referring to.

A mixologist who has engaged customers has more opportunities to learn about what those customers want and need. If the mixologist is working with productive people who are energized by the fact that they have engaged customers, they can help their companies create new solutions that satisfy customer needs and further engage them. This all makes flow easier.

The result is that the organization makes more money from keeping its customers and people engaged.

People are your power.

The Bits That Organizations Miss—People and Processes

You may be reading this and thinking I'm not telling you anything you don't already know. And you're right. As organization leaders, we know that engagement is crucial to our success. We're bombarded with the types of rote statistics I shared earlier, with every voice that matters telling us that we need to keep our people engaged if we want higher productivity, happier customers, and more profits. This can send us to sleep as we have heard it all before. We also know that engaged people are more likely to accept the digital transformations we want to create. Engagement creates trust. It encourages a feedback loop that makes our people feel like they're part of the transformation, which enables the changes to occur in the first place.

Again, I'm not telling you anything that you don't already know.

And yet, there are two key pieces of the engagement puzzle that so many organizations miss. By missing these pieces, companies hold themselves back from creating true engagement. Those pieces are:

1. The Processes
2. The People Themselves (Customers and Colleagues).

Let's look at each of these pieces to see what we can do about putting them into place and avoid resistance to learning from engagement building up over time.

Piece #1—The Processes

Messy and overelaborate processes plague modern organizations.

The issue I had with British Gas's email is a perfect example. It was sent to me as part of an automated or departmental process that didn't really make any sense. The process didn't ensure that I had clear next steps to follow to get my boiler serviced. And the email itself was sent during a time when *it wasn't even possible* for me to get the service. So, we have an automated process that fell down, leading to me feeling less engaged with the organization (but it shows another problem of people under-resourcing compared to the quality they profess in their marketing, further eroding brand trust).

We see plenty of examples of messy processes when we put ourselves in the role of a customer for other organizations. Think about the number of times somebody has told you that they can't do something for you because it's "against organization policy." How many times have you heard that and wondered why the thing you want is against policy when other companies can offer it? These terrible processes lead to poor customer experiences. Inevitably, the customer disengages and opts to buy from an organization that has processes in place to serve their needs.

We can probably all agree that fixing these types of processes is a priority. And yet, so many companies still aren't doing it. In June 2020, The Institute of Customer Service released its annual UK Customer Satisfaction Index. They found that customer satisfaction was 1.2 points below what it had been in 2018. This is despite the fact that new digital technologies enable the creation of smoother processes that should keep customers happier. The March 2025 statistics from https://www.moreincommon.org.uk/our-work/polling-tables/march-2025-polling-tables/ for the 'Computer says no' category shows 25+% dissatisfaction with Customer Service in sectors with some competitive choice and 45+% dissatisfaction with government-related services. Progress doesn't seem an important ambition.

What we see with these messy processes is the result of the inside-out focus that we've discussed throughout this book. If you think inside-out, it seems very little will motivate you until perhaps your own job is threatened. The companies that create these processes focus on what they need instead of placing the customer at the center of their process creation. Again, we can see this with my

British Gas example. The organization needed me to schedule a boiler service, so they created a process to remind me that my boiler needed servicing. However, they didn't consider the mechanics of getting that service booked. Nothing in the email made it easy for me to take the next step. And again, the email arrived at a time when I couldn't even arrange the service that British Gas wanted me to arrange. Siloed thinking. It made me wonder whether there was just a regulatory target to contact customers rather than any interest in the outcomes for customers—this, of course, has short-term cost benefits.

The remedy to these types of processes is to take the Outside-In approach, which requires focusing on the customer and organization-wide alignment for longer-term sustainability. In terms of processes, the best way to do this is to map all of the possible journeys a customer may take through your organization. In doing this, you understand every stage of the journey, essentially the process you've created. You can see where your customers have to deal with the lack of flow you've probably created if you use the critique standards you would expect in your personal life.

Look for the pain points and the parts of the journey where people drop out. Customers disengage in these places, meaning those points could benefit from the customer-centric outside-in approach. Look at the width of your processes—are they too narrow to make sense to a customer wanting an outcome?

Tidying up your processes makes it easier for your customers to get what they need from your organization. Better yet, your people benefit from working with smoother processes that don't force them into a position where they have to deny a customer what they want because it's "against policy."

Most importantly, look at your communications and culture—when did you dehumanize common sense and make your people compliant slaves to processes?

Piece # 2—The People Themselves (Both Customers and Colleagues)

The critical mistake that organizations make with the people aspect of the puzzle is that they focus only on a single set of people. So many of us focus on keeping our chosen people happy that we lose sight of providing a product or service that our customers want because we're too dialed into pleasing our regular clique.

In the previous chapter, we covered aspects of this when discussing the differing perceptions of quality. We also examined how this mentality damages an organization's ability to serve its customers and adapt to its environment because it creates the inside-out approach that we're trying to avoid. And again, we've already established that providing people with an emotionally compelling reason to buy from us leads to the profits that we're chasing for our stakeholders.

You need to account for the emotions and differing
perceptions involved in purchasing decisions.

If you're not offering a reason for your customers to get emotionally invested in what you're doing, they will see their relationship with you as transactional. They're disengaged and have no anchor to you or basis for trust, which makes it so easy for them to switch to another provider. Where does that emotion come from?

It's something else that we've already discussed.

Your organization's values and purpose!

When your colleagues connect to the organization's purpose and core values, you end up with engaged people who are more capable of entering the flow state, which leads to higher productivity levels. When your customers connect to those same two things, you create the emotional engagement that results in existing customers staying and more new customers coming on board (particularly through referrals, which is the lowest-cost customer acquisition channel).

Confronting the Common Organizational Blockers to "Good Digital"

It should be obvious by now that your people are the key to good and successful digital. Engaging your people, both inside the organization and out, clears one of the critical blockers that prevents the implementation of digital. Engaged people empower your mixologists to do what they do best—come up with ideas that serve your customers while serving the organization.

However, disengaged people are not the only organizational blocker to good and successful digital. There are several more we need to consider when creating digital transformation.

Agile Boundaries

While we've already established the importance of agility in digital transformation, a couple of issues create boundary issues in Agile. Technology tools and costs can end up ring-fencing Agile in IT or product teams, leading to an organizational lack of alignment in priorities. This occurs, in part, because Agile evangelists tend to turn people off like all shouty people who forget the ratio of ears to mouth. The blocker here is the frequent organizational bias towards structures that makes everyone want to fix others rather than themselves. This runs counter to Agile philosophy and prevents the development of the flexibility required for good digital.

Business Cases

Organizations take a capital approach to making investment decisions, leading to the quantitative mentality we've already discussed being insufficient for digital, which is ever-evolving.

Service delivery is treated as capital equipment, creating the potential for digital entropy. Here, we see a bias toward control that limits the possibility of flow and is, therefore, counter-productive. There are a number of pointers in this book as to what should be in a good business case, including outside-in outcomes, sustainability plan for the technology, ROI in revenue as well as cost terms, risk of unintended consequences in other parts of the organizational flow, data plan to measure intended and unintended consequences, people plan to deliver and operate. The business case is an opportunity to thoughtfully consider the full Digital mix rather than focus on an ingredient.

Functional Structure

Power bases remain classically functional while not taking the power that a total service owner has into account. The result is that both the service and the customer get lost and fragmented inside the structure, which runs contrary to the outside-in and flow approach we want to take. This occurs because the organization's current functional expertise seeps so deeply into the organization's silos that it's difficult to break away from the structure already in place.

Reward

The issue is that we often define rewards and incentives by the simplest means possible. There is a natural bias towards cost, as we see with incentive schemes that reward people for lowering expenses or achieving high sales. While these targets are important, they make no allowances for digital ambition and the increased competitive space that digital has given us, and inadvertently, they tend to place a select few most clearly aligned to sales or finance on a pedestal. Those who humbly go about doing an amazing job get lost in the shuffle, with organizations failing to reward people who excel in ways that aren't simplistically related to cost. The absence of flow and alignment in organizations also boxes people into cost centers or revenue-generating centers—often with an apparent judgment that service delivery does not impact revenues.

Lack of Diversity of Thought

Functional leadership that fits into an organization's best practices gets recruited or promoted ahead of all else. This desire for conformity holds a lot of power, creating a situation where management is based on objectives rather than people and outcomes. This dedication to functionality leads to inertia, creating high change management overheads as the organization resists change due to its devotion to functionality. Simply put, an organization lacking diversity in thought will always struggle when it needs to introduce change. It is not enough to just recruit that diversity (whether demographic, neuro, personality, or any other). The organization has to find ways of working that blend people together, such as Agile DevOps or peoples' Belbin Team Roles work style preferences (https://www.belbin.com/about/belbin-team-roles) approaches to people mixology.

Meat Grinding Machine

New talent comes on board, bringing new ideas with them. Instead of being encouraged to share these ideas to aid in creating change, the talent is trained to fit into the existing structure's needs. The talent gets rewarded if they don't rock the boat, leading to fewer ideas getting shared over time and less interest in creating flow.

Does your people policy have a
Gardening or Butchering DNA?

Job/Role/Task/Grade Confusion

When roles become formal specifications, confusion arises. People aren't rewarded for the outcomes they create, which means they're less likely to try and rock the boat with new ideas. Rather, they get locked into organizational inflexibility based on straitjacket job specifications with such long lists of requirements that some deficiency can always be found. These role requirements are often also based on rear-view mirrors.

Fear and Insecurity

We see this arise as a result of the VUCA world that we discussed in the previous chapter. People inherently want stability, which means it's difficult for them to stare into the harsh economic reality that digital change is needed to properly meet the needs of customers. They struggle to adapt to the transparency, visibility, and ambiguity of Agile and digital, leading to a focus on loss aversion rather than change creation. They naturally dislike people who are different and may change the AS IS and force a Change Curve on them.

Essentials Inflation

Job specifications become superhuman lists of essential tasks. The critical problem here is that these lists tend to focus on activity or toolset competencies rather than outcome competencies. This enhances organizational rigidity by tying rewards to compliance with existing systems and structures. Of course, those who would explore outside of these structures receive no rewards, regardless of outcomes, making them less likely to explore in the future. Long-term value can often be blocked by trainable checklist barriers.

Paint By Numbers

Skill does not come from the "paint by numbers" approach of indoctrinating people into the systems and functions that already exist in an organization. It comes from direction, momentum, learning by doing, encouragement, strategy, desire, and confidence. It is not possible to become confident when you feel like you have to refer to a manual to ensure you're doing things the "correct" way. The "paint by numbers" approach forces people to stay within the lines of what already exists instead of exploring what could be.

Foundation/Perfection

If only we had, and I invite you to <insert tool here>, we could achieve so much more.

If you've heard this inside your organization, it suggests that you promote for authority and mastery in function. Often, these two things are not driven by your desired outcome. What you end up building is based on who wins the arguments related to what you should build and when. You end up with a culture of controlling behavior in which your freethinkers (i.e., your mixologists) are not able to truly connect with customer needs. In Digital, there is also sometimes the bizarre notion that software "wears out" like tread on a tire—rather than being honest that much obsolescence is related to human capital and the persuasiveness of salespeople.

Lack of Organization Nous

It doesn't seem difficult to understand that providing products and services that people want and evolving solutions as needs mature while applying thought to innovation should lead to profit or progress. It's obvious. It's easy. Yet, organizations make things far too complex instead of focusing on doing the basics well.

Help Your People to Perform

I'll say it again: Your people are your power. We all know that engaging our customers and our colleagues is critical to the success of our organizations. However, too few take the active steps needed to maintain this engagement. They don't evolve with the times and leverage digital as the tool that enables and empowers engagement.

That's how organizations end up in a state of inertia. Too many blockages exist that prevent their people from caring about the organization. Customers have little emotional reason to stick with the organization, in addition to often getting tied up in messy processes created by poor digital implementation. Colleagues end up demotivated and less productive because they see customer disengagement and feel they're working without a purpose. Inertia becomes entrenched due to fear of marketing by vendors.

The thing is that it's not hard to overcome these problems.

Many people believe that digital means complex. They don't realize that digital is the tool they can use to get back to the basics of engaging customers and motivating colleagues. By focusing on those two fundamentals of an organization, you can leverage digital technology to truly take advantage of the power of your people.

CHAPTER SIX

It's Time to Create Change

There's a cocktail bar that I've been going to for about a year now.

It's called Urban Bar and I fell in love with it when I first discovered it. The music fits the mood and there were always plenty of patrons knocking back tasty cocktails. In addition to the perfect atmosphere, it also had a fantastic mixologist.

For a while, I couldn't get enough of the place.

But that was a year ago.

In that year, the bar hasn't changed a bit. It still looks exactly as it always did. The same music plays every single night and the whole atmosphere is starting to feel a little stagnant. What's more, there's another bar, called The Blue Bar, that has opened just down the road. This new bar has become the cool new hangout spot for a lot of the people who used to go to Urban Bar. Every time I head inside the Urban Bar, I notice that there are fewer people than there were during my last visit. And honestly, I have one foot out of the door myself. I've even spoken to the mixologist to let them know that their talents are going to waste at Urban Bar when The Blue Bar offers them the atmosphere and clientele they need to thrive in their role.

What we see here is a classic case of inertia. We don't accept it in our personal lives as much as in our work lives.

We've touched on this concept a few times already throughout the book. Here, Urban Bar's refusal to change, particularly in the face of energetic competition from The Blue Bar, places it in a constant state of inertia. Everything about the bar feels stale, old hat, lazy, and just a little bit boring—what was once fresh is now old. Inevitably, even Urban Bar's most loyal customers, such as myself, are going to want to leave because there's a new bar in town that offers a much more exciting and enriching service.

This is the danger of maintaining the status quo. And it applies to your organization just as much as it applies to Urban Bar. By trying to stay the same, no matter what your industry and customers are telling you, your organization enters inertia and begins to stagnate. While your competitors start to embrace and enjoy digital, using it to deliver what their customers want in the process, you get left behind. Your mixologists all leave to embrace the new challenges that await them elsewhere and your inertia leads to stagnation, which ultimately results in the death of the organization.

> *My point is that the only way to move forward*
> *is to change.*

Again, I'm not telling you anything new here. You're exploring digital because you've identified this very fact yourself—and it is possibly the reason why you picked up this book. However, this chapter aims to hone in on the dangers of remaining static when all around you is changing. It will also help you to create the change that you need to see to ensure that inertia doesn't claim yet another victim.

The Organization Laws of Physics

In life, there are immutable laws of physics that we all must follow, whether we want to or not. The law of gravity keeps us pinned to the Earth, and it makes sure that we come crashing down to Earth with a bang if we try to break it. Even things we've built to circumvent this law, such as airplanes, can only stay in the sky for so long before they come down. Gravity is an undeniable law of physics that we must all follow.

Of course, many more laws of physics exist. But why am I telling you this?

In organization, just as in life, there are laws of physics that we are all bound to. If we see physics as the science behind energy and matter, we can consider leadership as the principles and methods that we use to apply this science to our organizations. Lex Sisney first developed the laws I will introduce in his book *Organizational Physics: The Science of Growing an Organization*. Each is an inescapable law that you must both understand and follow as an organization leader. They are as follows:

Law #1—Organizations Are Adaptive Systems

An organization that thrives is one that is capable of adapting to the environment that it finds itself in. We have already discussed these types of concepts when examining agility in an organization environment. An organization incapable of adapting will eventually fall behind the pack and perish. Perhaps we can brutally refer to this as survival of the fittest in the organization world.

Those who do not adapt do not survive.

Law #2—All Organizations Are Subject to the First Law of Thermodynamics

The first law of thermodynamics tells us that every system has a finite amount of energy. Take our brief airplane example from above. A plane can break the laws of gravity for as long as there is fuel in its tanks. Once that finite source of energy is depleted, the plane will descend regardless of the actions of the pilot.

Now, let's look at what energy is from the perspective of your organization.

Your energy is your most talented employee. It's also your financial capital, your branding, and your position in the market. To create incremental energy, which is energy that moves you forward and unlocks creative innovation, you must align these sources of energy with the opportunities your market presents. Failure to achieve that alignment leads to your energy running out and Flow ceasing. Cash reserves get depleted, good people leave the organization, and the organization enters a state of inertia caused by not having the energy needed to propel itself forward. Employees also have a bunch of motivations that drive their energy levels.

When was the last time you delivered something creative? Do you like the answer?

Law #3—The Second Law of Thermodynamics Also Applies to Organizations

Everything deteriorates over time.

This process called entropy applies to everything, living or otherwise, in the universe. Nothing in this world can exist in the same state that it is currently in for an infinite amount of time. It will eventually decline, wither, and decay, be that a fast process or one that takes millennia.

The only way to combat entropy is to have energy and maintain flow. As entropy increases, so does the amount of energy needed to fight back against it. In an organizational sense, an organization in entropy has started to die. Of course, expending the energy reserves you have to keep that organization alive when it is in entropy brings you right back to the second law of organization physics.

Eventually, the energy runs out and entropy takes hold.

Law #4—Organizations Respond to Their Environments

If a gust of wind blows past your head, it catches your hair (assuming you're lucky enough to have any). If it starts to rain, you get wet. My point is that your body responds to the environment that you place it in. You may then take your responses further, such as using an umbrella to prevent the rain from soaking you or wearing a hat to stop the wind from messing up your hair.

Organizations are affected by their environments, just as we are.

Sisney identifies four key forces that impact an organization's environment, causing it to respond:

1. Innovation
2. Production
3. Stabilization
4. Unification.

Each of these forces interacts with one another inside your organization. Failure to understand this and an inability to govern and strengthen these forces create an environment in which you cannot see how your organization needs to change. You can't respond because you don't know what you're responding to!

Law #5—Organizations Follow the Laws of Evolution

Perhaps we're dipping into some biological laws here, in addition to physics laws. If a body responds to its environment, that response dictates whether it survives. In a biological sense, that response may be to adapt to the environment, which leads to evolution over time.

Again, we adapt to survive.

The most adaptive creatures stand the test of time. Those that fail to adapt to the environment are lost to the ages.

The same goes for organizations. We only need to look at the stories of major corporate beasts like Blockbuster and Kodak to see how failing to adapt to the environment leads to the collapse of organization monoliths. Interestingly, both of these companies were felled by their inability to adapt to digital technology.

Law #6—All Organizations Must Follow the Laws of Motion

It's here where we come back to our core concept of inertia.

To overcome inertia, a body must expend energy to create movement. When you walk, your brain sends signals to the muscles in your legs to conduct the walking motion. Those muscles need fuel to sustain that motion, which you receive from food. What's more, your muscles are subject to short-term entropy. They get tired, requiring more energy to keep going as time goes on. Eventually, your muscles will no longer be able to carry you forward, leading to inertia.

As we've seen with the previous laws, the same energy-based concepts relate to our organizations. If we don't have the energy, be that from people, capital, or whatever other resources we have, to keep moving, we will stop and enter a state of inertia.

This becomes a real challenge when you're trying to introduce change. Any form of transformation requires a great deal of energy expenditure. In an organizational sense, you spend this energy to overcome the fear that your people have about change. You spend it on training, innovating, and implementing. And just as we see with the human body and movement, the rate of change slows to a crawl if you don't have the energy required to sustain motion.

Still, motion is the only thing that allows us to overcome the inertia problem. However, inertia is also a problem that is as psychological as it is physical.

The Psychological Inertia Problem

An object at rest remains at rest, and an object in motion remains in motion unless acted upon by an outside force.

This is Newton's First Law of Motion, which we can also refer to as the law of inertia. And in a physical sense, we see how this law is true in every aspect of our lives. I've already offered several examples when speaking of the physics of organization, so I won't dig too much into them again here. Still, we all understand, on a fundamental level, that some sort of external force is required to either stop or move an object.

But what if that object is the mind?

This is where we get into something less tangible, as the mind is not a physical object that we can influence through force alone. And yet, it is just as possible for our minds to end up in an inert state as it is for any physical body.

We call this psychological inertia, and it is one of the largest barriers to change that your organization faces.

Psychological inertia refers to our desire to maintain the status quo in whatever situations we find ourselves in. And again, we see examples of this in all aspects of our lives. We follow certain routines because they bring us comfort. We avoid doing things that lie outside of our comfort zones because doing those things requires us to create a change of some description. In our organizations, we see psychological inertia in action every time an employee goes back to their rut by using an old method of doing things or whenever we face resistance to the change we're trying to create.

The true danger of psychological inertia is that it's not selective. Where status quo bias, which is very similar, leads us to avoid changes that we believe may lead to a loss of some description, psychological inertia causes us to avoid *all change*. It doesn't matter if there are logical arguments to demonstrate why that change is both beneficial and necessary. People with psychological inertia are happy right where they are, thank you very much, and they're not going to change just because logic seems to suggest they should.

Of course, this becomes especially frustrating to organization owners and leaders when they're trying to create change in their organizations. Psychological inertia is the enemy of innovation. It prevents you from creating a culture of mixology because it is the exact opposite of what that type of culture represents. It's the reason why Urban Bar refuses to change, even though the owners can see that The Blue Bar is going to swallow up all of their clientele if they do not change.

Psychological inertia is a dangerous and insidious thing.

And that leads us to a question:

How do we overcome psychological inertia?

A little later in this chapter, I'll offer some of my own insights into what you must do to enable change in your organization. Here, I'll refer to the work of Lamar University's Lynn Godkin and University of New England's Seth Allcorn. In their paper, *Overcoming Organizational Inertia: A Tripartite Model for Achieving Strategic Organizational Change,* the duo dive into detail about how psychological inertia forms and the effects that it can have on an organization. However, they also highlight three critical "Promoters of Change" that you may be able to use to overcome inertia in your organization.

Change Promoter #1—Acquiring Insight

A lack of organizational insight can lead to the development of inertia. Godkin and Allcorn discuss two techniques to overcome this issue: Double Loop Learning and Reflective Practice.

Double Loop Learning allows us to revisit the issues related to bias that we examined in the book's first two chapters. This technique involves examining the underlying reasons behind your behavior or that of your team. What misconceptions, distortions, and supposed understanding of your environment lead to the decision to remain inert? Through Double Loop Learning, you question the actions and practices you have always followed while also examining, and often overruling, the assumptions that led to establishing these practices in the first place.

Building on this, we also have reflective practice. Here, we learn from our own experiences, in addition to the experiences of others, to determine an appropriate course of action. In other words, we reflect on what we know to provide us with insight into where we need to go. The point about using the experiences of others is critical here. Inertia often occurs when leaders rely on their own experiences alone when making decisions related to their organizations. By examining and learning from the experiences of others, you develop another tool for creating insight without being swayed by your personal biases.

Change Promoter #2—Focusing on Action

No matter how much information you gather, it never seems enough. You need to learn more and more and more, constantly chasing a perfect representation of the situation before you finally make a decision. Of course, we can never have enough information, especially in a digital world where data is constantly generated. So, this desire to collect every piece of information possible is essentially another form of psychological inertia. We chase perfection despite knowing it is not possible, which leads to a lack of action because we're still gathering information.

Does that sound familiar?

It will be to anybody who has hemmed and hawed (https://en.wikipedia.org/wiki/Who_Moved_My_Cheese) over a decision for months on end, always wanting to know one more thing before they take the plunge one way or the other.

Godkin and Allcorn recommend making action a core focus for an organization to overcome this aspect of psychological inertia. They provide an example of forming cross-functional groups. Through these types of groups, leaders can gather insights and highlight action items that they may not have identified based on their own assumptions. Cross-functional groups serve to highlight the dangerous assumptions that often lead to inertia while allowing for an organization to take swift action.

They also point to developing a systematic approach to problem-solving as critical to ensuring swift action that counters inertia. By having a system, you also have a defined set of steps to follow during the information-gathering process. Instead of trying to grab information from everywhere and anywhere, which leads to the desire to find more that so often causes inertia, you have a system that focuses your information-gathering activities so that what you collect serves the action you need to take.

Change Promoter #3—Confronting Your Own Resistance to Change

To create change in another person, you must first create change in yourself.

It's the sort of leadership theory that has existed for centuries, to the point where any organization leader will tell you that good leadership starts with a focus on self. However, we can also apply this simple theory to your own psychological readiness to change.

If you're suffering from psychological inertia, your people will suffer from it by proxy. Even your innovators, your mixologists, will be forcibly inert because you're keeping them at a standstill. Only by confronting your resistance to change can you create an environment where others can change, too, with a positive shadow of the leadership.

Think back to what I said about telling the mixologist at Urban Bar that they'd be well-served to ply their trade at The Blue Bar. The mixologist likely didn't need me to tell them that. They work at Urban Bar, which means they've seen the bar owner's resistance to change or lack of available investment funds first-hand. That resistance will lead to Urban Bar losing its mixologist, whether to The Blue Bar or somebody else. The mixologist may have had ideas and motivation to suggest change, but if the power base is inert, then in the end, they will give up.

Here, we want to focus on becoming enabling leaders. These types of leaders value collaboration and create environments in which their people feel safe to experiment and innovate. An enabling leader is not guided by their own biases, making them more susceptible to change. They overcome their own psychological inertia by welcoming diversity of opinions into the organization, thereby helping them gather insight they would not gather on their own.

As an organizational leader, change starts with you.

That is as true of the psychological change required to avoid inertia as it is of your actions to achieve that same goal. By the way—do you know what your change blockers are and where that baggage comes from? Time to move on!

The Five Steps for Creating Change (So You Can Deliver Value)

So, we have established that inertia exists on the psychological scale, just as it does on the physical. A mind cannot be in motion if we don't apply the psychological force needed to make it move, just as a physical body can't be in motion without some sort of force creating that motion.

Understanding this concept of psychological inertia brings us to yet another question:

What can we do to get our minds moving?

In other words, how can we overcome the psychological barriers to change, enabling ourselves and our people to be motivated to embrace and implement change? To answer this question, I have five steps that confront both the mental and organizational action aspects of overcoming inertia.

Step #1—Make Conscious Choices

You don't need me to continue prattling on about the role our unconscious biases play in our decision-making. I've covered it above and in earlier chapters. Still, it needs repeating here because the only way to overcome the unconscious aspects of our decision-making processes is to become conscious of our decision-making.

In her 2018 article, *The Power of Making a Conscious Choice*, Forbes Council Member Susan Taylor discusses how the decisions that small organization owners take can make or break them. As such, she implemented three criteria that help her to make conscious decisions about who she works with:

1. Is the person committed to positive change?

2. Is the person driven by a willingness to change their inner self to serve the greater good?

3. Is the person willing to break the status quo and push past any boundaries that prevent them from being a good client or partner?

In this example, Susan makes her decisions based on the values that she wants to instill in her organization. You will also notice that some of these values, such as the willingness to change and the desire to avoid the status quo, are values that oppose the inertia that we've spoken about in this chapter. Through this series of questions, Susan empowers herself to make a conscious decision about how her organization moves forward based on the values that she wants the organization to have rather than on any unconscious influences that may otherwise guide her.

Even if Susan's conscious questions don't perfectly reflect what you're hoping to achieve through digital change, the concept behind them offers insight into overcoming resistance to said change. This is all about taking knee-jerk, reactionary, and unconscious decision-making off the table, replacing it instead with a conscious examination of the decision in question. By being conscious of our choices, we enable ourselves to reflect on them and understand why we make the decisions we typically make. By doing this, we take a crucial step towards creating change as we begin to overcome the unconscious biases that had previously prevented change.

Step #2—Accept That There Are Unknowns (and Do Something About Them)

In Chapter Two, we discussed the concept of our knowns and unknowns at length. To summarize, we have:

- Known knowns
- Known unknowns
- Unknown knowns
- Unknown unknowns.

It's this last one that is particularly dangerous from a change perspective. When we know what our unknowns are, we are at least conscious of what we need to focus on to create change.

However, the unknown unknowns are more insidious because they affect what we do without us even realizing they exist.

We want to bring those unknown unknowns to light.

To do that, you can use three strategies:

1. Seek the perspective of an insider who can help you to shed light on whatever you don't know. Digital change offers a perfect example here. By consulting with a creative digital mixologist, you learn more about the challenges you must overcome to make digital change possible. These challenges are often your unknown unknowns simply because you do not have prior experience with digital to gain wisdom from.

2. Conduct a premortem on the change you want to create. This is an interesting concept that assumes that your action failed. In your premortem, you'll outline all of the potential reasons for that hypothetical failure. By doing this, you become a devil's advocate to yourself, overcoming the natural bias you have towards assuming you will succeed in the process. This is an ideal exercise to involve your team in, as your people may see ways that an organization's action may fail that you may be blind to. Clearly, this needs to be positioned in the positive context of overcoming barriers to change!

3. Test yourself for implicit assumptions at every turn. Again, this revisits our concept of trying not to do things

in a certain way simply because "that's the way we've always done them." That mindset is the very root of organizational inertia, which means we have to challenge it constantly. When planning your digital change, look for areas of the plan where you repeat processes or implement systems that already exist in your organization. Ask yourself if you're doing that because the process or system is ideal or if you're doing it because it's the way you've always done it. You may have an implicit assumption to overcome if it's the latter.

Step #3—Build a Minimum Viable (Sellable/Useful) Product and Iterate From It using factual data

In some cases, change resistance occurs because the sheer scale of the product or change intimidates an organization. This is where building a minimum viable product (MVP) becomes useful. An MVP is the most stripped-back version of your product, app, software, or digital offering that you can offer to the consumer. The idea is to release the MVP to essentially test the market and ensure there is demand for whatever you're offering. With demand established, you can then combine your assumptions about the product with the feedback and data you receive from early adopters to iterate on the MVP, building it up to the point where it becomes a full consumer product.

So, you build a product to test your biggest assumptions and features. Then, you add all of the bells and whistles to it over time, as the product gains traction and you get more feedback from the consumer base.

This makes the change less intimidating while also helping you develop a roadmap for future development, which provides clarity for the product's future. Note: an MVP is not the same as making it up as you go along—which is a lazy agile trap.

Step #4—Investment Choices and Sourcing Strategy

Fundamentally, most organizations have low digital situational awareness and low numbers of people with the required perspective. The result is that we tend to make investment and strategy decisions based on tools like SWOT analysis, which often fail to provide us with the full picture of a situation.

In his keynote speech *Situation Normal, Everything Must Change*, Open Europe Fellow and Wardley Mapping founder Simon Wardley provides an interesting example of what this can look like in practice. He references the famous battle of the 300 Spartans, initially using a physical map to outline the strategy the Spartans will follow in their battle against the Persians. He then compares this to a SWOT analysis of that same battle, which outlines the strengths, weaknesses, opportunities, and threats most relevant to the battle.

He then asks which of the two would be most effective in combat.

The Map.

What do we use in an organization?

The SWOT.

The point is that we base so many of our strategy and investment decisions on tools that fail to show us the true lie of the land. This moves us away from playing with intelligence, which is one of the cores of mixology, and towards making analog decisions based on a few bullet points.

This does not work for digital.

Digital is ever-evolving due to customer cause-and-effect iterations. In other words, the map of the battlefield changes constantly as customer needs evolve and we react to them. The problem is that we're still working from analog "maps," such as SWOT, instead of recognizing that digital has many more depths and dimensions that we can only confront with an appropriate map. This focus on the analog is what leads to companies dabbling in digital. In the digital world, time moves faster, commoditization is more savage, and new ideas spread at a rate that we never saw in the analog world. To keep up, you cannot take an analog approach. You must play with intelligence by embracing mixology so you can answer the fundamental questions that inform digital strategy:

Where would you invest?

Are you clear about what is a tool compared to what is a service or offering that is close to your customer?

Do you know how your customers score their priorities in comparison to your own internal scoring? We focused on this question before when we discussed the potential differences between a customer's idea of quality and an organization's ideas. To put it another way—can you align your value proposition and the way you deliver it to the customer's perceptions of value? Ask yourself who is going to give you money. Of course, it's the customer.

It is also worth looking at Simon Wardley's mapping, in particular, to consider likely rates of commoditization, who may commoditize, and in what direction. This risk (and maybe benefit) of commoditization should be considered in terms of the sustainability of your digital investment and ROI horizon (https://www.wardleymaps.com/).

Build close to the customer to avoid creating a product that the wider market will quickly commoditize. To do that, you must embrace that you're not working on an analog basis anymore.

Are you comfortable that your digital is sustainable or easily swappable?

Step #5—Understand How Much Value Your Product Needs to Deliver When You Finish Iterating

The customer is the key to your organization's success.

Not you. Not your competition. The customer is the one who determines the standards of quality and what your product needs to offer them in order for them to stick with you.

This is the core theme of the entire book. We have repeatedly tackled the idea of working from the inside out and how encouraging an outside-in approach that focuses on delivering value to your customers is the way to go.

In the case of creating change, your customers are the critical component. What are they telling you about the value that your product needs to deliver by the time you finish iterating? Follow the roadmap they provide, and you'll be much more likely to execute digital change successfully.

Of course, this brings us back to the seemingly intangible concept of value. We all understand what we mean when we talk about the price of the products we create. However, we also cannot assume that the price we pay represents the value we receive. For strategic purposes, you need to consider the value your product offers for the price you're charging for it. This is a far less tangible concept, as value is determined by the customer's perception of the quality of the product, as we established earlier in the book.

We can think of value in simple pricing terms:

A product's value is the largest amount of money a customer will pay for the product. As such, in the customer's perception, a product that offers little value for the price being charged will not get bought. By contrast, a product that appears to offer more value than the price suggests will get bought in droves.

Why does all of this talk of price and value matter so much?

For customers, the interplay between price and value is what they pay attention to when making purchasing decisions. As organization leaders, we need to ensure that interplay leads to our products offering what the customer wants while also ensuring that we don't damage our organizations in the process.

And this brings us back to the idea of iteration. You could iterate a piece of software so much that you end up providing a ton of value in the eyes of your customers. But if you offer that value at a low price, you may fail to reclaim the investment made in iterating the product. That means you need to strike a balance between how much value your product offers and what you charge people for access to that product. The failure to strike this balance again leads to change resistance, as people inside your organization see that you're offering too much for too little (or too little for too much) and push against the direction you're going in.

So, we again find ourselves asking a question that we've asked several times before.

What does the customer see as valuable?

Answer that and you can focus on developing a change strategy that delivers that value while making logical sense to all your organization's stakeholders.

Organize for Success

So, how do we organize our companies for digital success?

Every choice you make and every design you work on is linked to your organization's strategic architecture. At the bottom of this architecture, you have the places where you source your digital solutions, whether they be data, technology, services (or bits of them). These are typically your suppliers. You need to build the capability to source the appropriate digital solutions, which extends far beyond the procurement aspect. The key to mixology is that you find ways to differentiate pieces of the digital solution so you don't end up building a commodity that will get swallowed up in the market.

You may have noticed that I introduced the word *architecture*. You wouldn't build property without a design, so don't do digital with a build first and see what we end up with approach either. That said, all architects are divas, so make sure you get what you need.

For example, a streaming service that offers exactly what Netflix offers isn't going to make a dent in the market. You're creating a commodity that already exists, which means it offers no value to the customer.

So, we see sourcing as a key aspect of organizing for success. But what else is involved?

You need to manage your investments effectively. Going digital consumes time, money, resources, etc., which reduces opportunities elsewhere. You need to understand what you're giving up and why, so you can confirm that the digital change you hope to create is the optimal choice for your organization.

You also need to understand process design, both from an internal perspective and in terms of the processes you develop that relate to your customers. Again, we see the outside-in approach here. Your customers dictate the value of your product, which means they affect how you organize your delivery of that product. This feeds into designing the customer experience, as you also need to be clear about the feelings you want to create with your digital solution. How are you going to differentiate it? How does the solution offer value that the customer can't get elsewhere, thus (thereby) ensuring you don't end up delivering a commodity? How will the product you build create the customer loyalty that drives revenue?

And finally, you need a plan to implement organizational change. That's the subject that we have focused on throughout this chapter. You need to change your organization to fit the digital art of the possible rather than the pragmatic. It's here where your mixologists come to the fore, as it is their job to guide your people into moving beyond the organizational inertia and natural entropy that affects all organizations.

Your mixologists don't break the laws of organization physics.

However, they certainly play a huge role in slowing them down or making them work in your favor. Your mixologists create momentum through innovation, which enables the execution of organizational change.

Organization in Practice (and How the Digital Mixologist Hangs Everything Together)

We've covered the general aspects of organizing an organization for digital. However, perhaps what I've described above can be better represented in a diagram demonstrating how a digital organization looks in practice.

I happen to have such a diagram (co-created with Chris Potts), and it doesn't look like a hierarchical functional organizational chart (see the following page).

It looks a little intimidating, doesn't it? This one covers a B2B2C (Business to Business providing Consumer services) and in a Group company context.

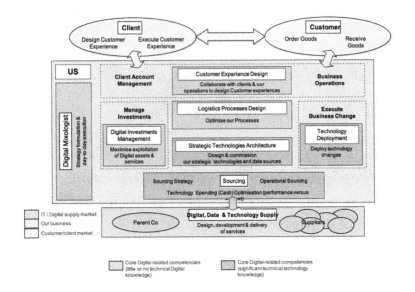

Let's break this diagram down into some of its core components so we can examine exactly what we need for each.

Customer Experience Design

You may have clients, customers, partners, or a combination of the three. Each has its own needs as they relate to the digital product you create and, indeed, your organization as a whole. You need to develop a capability inside your organization that allows you to determine and design to those needs. We see our ideas about value coming to the fore again here. The needs reflect the value that the client, customer, or partner hopes to receive from you. It's your duty to develop an experience that offers the value required to meet the need.

Operations

The operations aspect of your organization focuses on delivering the day-to-day experience the product offers based on the processes you define. Of course, those processes, as we established earlier, are based on what the customer wants. By taking the outside-in approach we've spoken about throughout the book, you can develop processes to ensure your organization's operations deliver a digital offering that brings value to the customer. Base your internal productivity key performance indicators on these processes and you're on to becoming an operational structure winner.

Account Management

Far too often, we see account management focused on executing processes. This approach leads to customer frustration, as the customer is told something "can't be done" because the process for doing it doesn't exist.

I'm not claiming that processes aren't important to successful account management here. However, we must focus on executing the experience in addition to following the processes we have in place. Remember that the experience defines the processes. If the experience gets damaged because a process isn't in place to deliver said experience, that's a sign that you need to revisit the processes you've created for account management.

Direction and Investment

An organization's direction should be defined in a documented game plan, which you could refer to as a target organization architecture, target operating model, and organization plan if you prefer frameworks. Of course, following that direction requires suitable investment. Make your investment choices consciously from the field of choices available to you rather than making your decisions in isolation. Here, we see the concepts of encouraging external insight that helps you to discover your blind spots and unknown unknowns come into play. Every iteration of your digital solution has to move you towards the overall game plan. And that game plan is determined both by what you learn from your customers and what your team can show you about where you need to invest.

Sourcing

Rather than focusing solely on screwing down costs for the commodities you buy, work on finding capability through your sourcing. This requires a little organization and mixology savvy, as the price will always be a factor when sourcing materials, technology, and software. You need to understand when to innovate and when to focus solely on the price. After all, innovation will lead you nowhere if you bankrupt your organization in the pursuit of it.

The Mixologist Hangs Everything Together

Digital isn't just a change in terms of the specific product that your organization offers to consumers. It should change everything about your organization, from the experience you offer to your internal measures, functional responsibilities, and the processes you use as the foundation of your operations.

You need people who understand the subtlety of well-formed change over time, rather than those who push for drastic one or two-dimensional change that affects the product but doesn't lead to change within the organization. A focus on all dimensions of digital is required to achieve the profound benefits of being an outside-in organization that is capable of executing a conscious digital game plan.

This is where your mixologists become crucial to your success.

It's your mixologists who hang all of this together through their deeper understanding of digital and their ability to encourage change at an organizational level. They're the ones who can measure your capabilities, see where you're steering away from the customer experience and towards the internal, and who provide the impetus for starting your digital journey.

They implement the cycle of digital, which makes them essential for bringing every aspect of this organizational model together.

Getting Some Quick Wins

We've tackled some broad and difficult topics in this book. Perhaps one of the critical messages from your reading experience is that "going digital" is not something you can do with the flick of a switch. It's a process that requires a proper and motivated approach to customers, organizational structure, and change management to create digital flow. You will face many challenges and obstacles on the road, meaning digital transformation takes time and a concerted effort to create a cultural change overcoming the many causes of inertia.

You may feel a little wary of the scale of the task.

That's why I want to round off this chapter with a few quick wins you can make in your organization today. What I'm about to share won't create the full digital transformation you seek. But, by implementing these action steps, you place yourself on the road to creating an organization that can embrace digital, understand its many dimensions, and empower your mixologists to do what they do best. It will help get a little mixology mojo going.

Your Digital Organization Rules of Thumb

We can use six rules of thumb to determine if our digital change efforts feel right. They are as follows:

1. List everything that you're currently buying to enable the change and plot them on two axes with a 1–10 scale. The

axes are "Rate of Commoditization" and "Direct Value to Customer." If you don't know the answers, bring some of your people into the mix to provide them. This enables you to see the true longevity of the features you're creating so you can determine how (and if) digital supports revenue generation—and it is also a good indicator of what you should build or buy.

2. Have your digital people list all of your solution's code chunks and then give them a rating from 1 to 10 based on whether the chunk will be unique in two years and if it offers value to the customer. This will give you an indication of whether your digital team is pushing the competitive edge, having poverty of ambition, or doing that IT scorched earth/not invented here thing.

3. Have whoever is in charge of your digital service releases create a list of all releases from the last six months. Score those releases based on their expected and actual value to customers, utilization, and feedback derived. This will help you see if you're releasing useful and useful things or if your prioritization is internally biased and unambitious. This is not a blame thing—it is a learning thing. Does your strategy have any discernible quality of ambition?

4. Stick your job specifications in a word cloud and examine what pops up. Do the words shout "customer," "outcomes," or "flexibility" to you? If not, you may need

to work on the latent mindset that underpins your organization and its hiring efforts.

5. Facilitate unfiltered customer contact. Regularly listen to calls, allow about 5% of emails to go out with a "please reply" email address, and listen to the transcripts that come from your chatbots or voice recognition systems. This gives you a reality check in terms of what your customers are seeing and getting from the product. Are you proud of what you hear?

6. Review your business case template against the values in this book. Honestly appraise whether they will aid or kill the digital you want.

Situation Analysis

Is your organization prepared for the organizational alignment challenges that come with digital? These four actions help you to find out.

1. Hire a digital mixologist to conduct an audit on your delivery alignment as it relates to your organization's strategy. Think about this in terms of having somebody come in to pick out all of the gaps in your enterprise value. What would that person find? By filling these gaps, you ensure your digital will meet your organization's strategy. Focus on the broad strokes—

don't grind down your team morale with death by a thousand audit minutiae.

2. Conduct an agile productivity audit. Perception of productivity is a serious challenge when it comes to the agile approach. Consider service orientation, product ownership, strategy, and ethos when conducting this audit. This will help you to see where delivery is going to give you a return.

3. Write down your organization strategy for digital in plain speak—run it through some grammar software to test for clarity. Personally, give it to some of your customers, employees, and friends in a cocktail bar (one that has a mixologist, of course). Encourage your management team to do the same. If the feedback you get tells you that your approach to digital doesn't carry much clear profound meaning to your customers and employees, then your approach may be too generic, sterile or buzzwordtastic to ensure your digital offering doesn't become commoditized.

4. Create an advisory board filled with people who you know will tell you what they think because they have little to lose. Listen to these people because they'll give insight that you may not get from those inside the organization who do have something to lose by speaking up. No, I don't mean recruiting non-executives from the

"right" backgrounds recruited by risk-avoiding executive recruitment search firms.

Getting Serious

When you're ready to get really serious with digital, three actions give you some further wins:

1. Put together a team that is focused on digital but *is not* filled solely with technology people. Appoint a leader from outside the technology arm of the organization, such as somebody in Sales, Marketing, or HR. This enables you to work *on* the organization and work *around* the core digital delivery to facilitate productivity and agile outcomes.

2. Conduct some hardcore digital roadmap retrospectives. Your mixologist, an HR consultant, and perhaps even an agile coach can facilitate this retrospective. The benefit here is that you have a process that helps you work on the organization rather than using people who are not normally in the agile machinery. These retrospectives build trust in digital because they help you identify the useful, usable, and used stuff that demonstrates that digital is worth your time.

3. Make people feel safe and commit to providing meaningful roles in the new transformed organization. Remove the inter-generational trauma, like the fear that

you see them as a cost that has not yet been automated or digitized out yet. They will then contribute or at least lower the inertia.

It's Time to Enjoy Digital

Digital is not something to fear. Remember, while people can often be scared of change, they generally would like to deliver value out of self-respect, at least. I believe the marginal cost is low and the pride/morale and flow benefits are massive in delivering meaningful digital. Digital is something to relish and enjoy, in addition to being something that you need to embrace to avoid the commoditization of your services. Conducting digital change, particularly at an organizational level, does not have to be some frightening task that strikes fear in the hearts of your people. Instead, it's your route to staving off, and perhaps even overcoming, the operational inertia and entropy that affects *all* organizations. There is so much digital stuff out there that it should be as fun as being a kid in a sweet shop.

Let's make digital creative again.

As we reach the conclusion of this book, I'd like you to reflect on the concepts of Revology the book opened with and the mixology meme that we've spoken about at length. Neither requires an organization to change every aspect of itself. Instead, they often enable profound digital innovation through the reuse of many ingredients that you already have in place. Think of the mixologist behind the bar who has a whole heap of ingredients they use for a set list of cocktails. Within that ingredients list, there is room for experimentation and innovation beyond the cocktails that the bar already serves. We can see the possibility of innovation even when hard constraints exist.

The same applies to your organization. Of course, there are hard constraints that you will face when going digital. But you're on the right track if you see these constraints as opportunities to mix things up and challenge your soft skills. Draw from your skills, experience, and imagination. Encourage your people (especially your mixologists) to do the same. But equally, encourage the outside-in approach that allows you to draw from the insight and perceptions of your customers. After all, it's your customers who generate revenue for your organization. By ensuring they receive an offering that offers them the level of value they expect, you take big steps on the road to true digital success.

I'll leave you with a final message.

Don't spend all of your focus trying to make sure that digital doesn't go wrong. By doing that, you miss your opportunity to mix things up and create a flow that moves you in the right direction and creates that digital winners culture.

Get mixing – deliver more than the sum of the ingredients. Sláinte! Santé! Cin! Cin! Skål Prost Şerefe Salud Saúde Na Zdrowie chris@digitalmixologist.com

Helpful Resources

Chapter One

https://www.youtube.com/watch?v=74Xa3YUtp2Y&authuser=0

https://github.com/gchq/BoilingFrogs

https://revologycars.com/meet-the-team/

https://hbswk.hbs.edu/item/the-outside-in-approach-to-customer-service

https://blog.hypeinnovation.com/inside-out-versus-outside-in-whats-the-better-strategy#:~:text=The%20Inside%2DOut%20approach%20is,is%20the%20key%20to%20success.

https://customerthink.com/outside-in-vs-inside-out-thinking/

https://en.wikipedia.org/wiki/Pin_the_tail_on_the_donkey#:~:text=The%20blindfolded%20child%20is%20then,is%20only%20of%20marginal%20importance.

http://www.informatica.si/index.php/informatica/article/viewFile/25/20

https://www.batimes.com/articles/the-silver-bullet-syndrome.html

https://www.boardofinnovation.com/blog/16-cognitive-biases-that-kill-innovative-thinking/

https://understandinguncertainty.org/node/109

https://www.psychologytoday.com/gb/basics/groupthink

https://www.psychologytoday.com/gb/blog/science-choice/201504/what-is-confirmation-bias

https://www.idealrole.com/blog/affinity-bias

https://www.ideastogo.com/innovation-blog/conformity-bias-how-it-affects-innovation?rq=conformity%20bias

http://psyc604.stasson.org/Asch1956.pdf

https://hbr.org/2017/07/how-tribalism-hurts-companies-and-what-to-do-about-it

https://thinkingfocus.com/how-to-make-your-team-more-productive-start-with-your-shadow/

https://www.cipd.org/uk/knowledge/factsheets/pestle-analysis-factsheet/

https://www.forbes.com/advisor/investing/esg-investing/

https://www.lifehack.org/577203/the-purpose-listening-understand-not-reply

https://corpgov.law.harvard.edu/2020/07/14/maximizing-the-benefits-of-board-diversity-lessons-learned-from-activist-investing/

Chapter Two

http://www.spsp.org/news-center/blog/romanticconfidence#gsc.tab=0

https://www.drjimtaylor.com/4.0/

https://www.psychologytoday.com/gb/blog/science-made-practical/202006/how-reset-the-way-others-see-you-get-more-respect

Chapter Three

https://uxdesign.cc/the-knowns-and-unknowns-framework-for-design-thinking-6537787de2c5

https://www.scientificamerican.com/article/rumsfelds-wisdom/

https://www.nngroup.com/articles/service-design-101/

https://en.wikipedia.org/wiki/Service_design#:~:text=Service%20design%20is%20the%20activity,service%20provider%20and%20its%20users

https://hbr.org/1984/01/designing-services-that-deliver

https://www.mckinsey.com/organization-functions/operations/our-insights/the-human-factor-in-service-design

https://www.mckinsey.com/organization-functions/organization/our-insights/the-five-trademarks-of-agile-organizations

https://www.bain.com/insights/how-to-plan-and-budget-for-agile-at-scale/

https://www.scaledagileframework.com/capex-and-opex/

https://www.scaledagileframework.com/lean-budgets/

https://hbr.org/2011/12/the-power-of-collective-ambition

https://www.linkedin.com/pulse/digital-transformation-dead-john-lowe/?trackingId=5e7EsAsDT1OIM6AOR%2FoFeQ%3D%3D

Chapter Four

https://www.psychologytoday.com/gb/tests/career/success-likelihood-test

https://www.megalexis.com/en/blog/posts/2017/all/what-is-quality/

https://en.wikipedia.org/wiki/Eight_dimensions_of_quality

https://en.wikipedia.org/wiki/Primary/secondary_quality_distinction

https://www.toptal.com/designers/ux/design-process-objective-or-subjective

https://www.thespruceeats.com/what-is-mixology-759941

https://mixologyevents.co.uk/uncategorized/what-is-mixology/

https://www.barschool.com/whats-a-mixologist/

https://en.wikipedia.org/wiki/VUCA

https://www.vuca-world.org/

https://www.mindtools.com/pages/article/managing-vuca-world.htm

https://www.researchgate.net/publication/301215134_THE_THEORY_OF_FLOW_AND_ITS_RELEVANCE_FOR_ORGANIZATIONS_part1

https://medium.com/better-humans/the-managers-guide-to-cultivating-flow-at-work-f4480cfa85e2

https://www.tonyrobbins.com/mind-meaning/10-common-defense-mechanisms/

https://www.healthline.com/health/mental-health/defense-mechanisms

https://psychcentral.com/lib/15-common-defense-mechanisms/

Chapter Five

https://www.custerian.com/blog/successfully-engage-customers-and-realise-50percent-higher-productivity

https://outgrowco.medium.com/customer-engagement-statistics-in-2020-547e41c70c74

https://www.custerian.com/messy-processes-messy-customer-experiences/

https://www.instituteofcustomerservice.com/research-insight/ukcsi

Chapter Six

https://en.wikipedia.org/wiki/Psychological_inertia

http://journal.sjdm.org/jdm06002.pdf

https://www.forbes.com/sites/forbescoachescouncil/2018/11/02/the-power-of-making-a-conscious-choice/#50e57eb85536

https://hbr.org/2017/10/simple-ways-to-spot-unknown-unknowns

https://www.cobbleweb.co.uk/iterating-mvp/

https://www.youtube.com/watch?v=Ty6pOVEc3bA

https://www.youtube.com/watch?v=zqjnBlKM5sU

https://www.mckinsey.com/organization-functions/strategy-and-corporate-finance/our-insights/delivering-value-to-customers

Index

Achilles' heal, 33

adversity, 69, 71, 74

affinity bias, 45, 47

Agile, 118, 119, 124, 129, 131, 186, 188, 190

agility, 108, 117, 118, 124, 145, 186, 196

Amazon, 15

Ambiguity, 140

arrogance, 62, 63, 64, 90

Asch Conformity Test, 47

Asch, Solomon E., 47

B2B. See Business to Business

Belbin Team Roles, 188

Best Buy, 15, 16, 20

Business to Business, 177, 219

CFO, 59

cocktail bar, 58, 59, 60, 64, 76, 81, 82, 87, 124, 171, 172, 193, 227

Complexity, 140

confidence, 54, 55, 58, 59, 60, 61, 62, 63, 64, 65, 66, 67, 68, 69, 70, 71, 72, 73, 74, 75, 76, 77, 78, 95, 119, 132, 144, 165, 190

configuration, 81

Conscious Competence Learning Model, 88

COO, 46

culture, 12, 13, 14, 23, 28, 29, 30, 95, 144, 149, 160, 161, 164, 167, 172, 184, 191, 202, 230

customer engagement, 177, 178, 179

data integration, 81

denial, 159

Design a Service, 109

digital cocktail, 11

digital mixologist, 11, 14, 51, 53, 155, 172, 173, 210, 226

digital product, 79, 83, 87, 102, 220

digital project, 10, 76, 87, 102

digital solution, 77, 81, 83, 84, 85, 87, 88, 98, 99, 101, 102, 103, 106, 107, 140, 146, 217, 218, 222

digital transformation, 56, 74, 98, 129, 130, 131, 146, 147, 148, 152, 154, 157, 159, 160,

161, 162, 164, 166, 168, 173, 186, 224

director, 46

Double Loop Learning, 203

drinkologist, 51, 54

Easterbrook, Steve, 16

enterprise, 1, 2, 120, 226

Federal Motor Vehicle Safety Standards, 8

flow, 60, 101, 121, 122, 145, 146, 147, 148, 149, 150, 151, 152, 153, 154, 155, 156, 157, 158, 168, 169, 170, 177, 178, 180, 183, 185, 187, 188, 189, 197, 224, 230, 233

FMVSS. See Federal Motor Vehicle Safety Standards

Ford Mustang, 6

Four Seasons Hotels, 125

GFC. See Global Financial Crisis

Global Financial Crisis, 125

going digital, 54, 224, 230

Goldman Sachs, 30

Gulati, Ranjay, 15

inertia, 1, 2, 12, 14, 23, 25, 26, 28, 32, 34, 35, 46, 48, 51, 56, 110, 111, 129, 157, 159, 168, 188, 192, 194, 195, 197, 199, 200, 201, 202, 203, 204, 205,

206, 207, 208, 211, 219, 224, 229, 234

innovation, 1, 2, 13, 17, 30, 46, 109, 119, 131, 191, 197, 202, 219, 222, 230

inside-out, 19, 21, 22, 24, 29, 36, 37, 40, 50, 54, 55, 56, 85, 87, 102, 109, 159, 170, 175, 182, 184, 231

Kahneman, Daniel, 33

Khoury, Salim, 82

known knowns, 96, 102, 103

known unknowns, 96, 101

Landaw, Jared, 46

leaders, 2, 3, 9, 25, 27, 29, 30, 41, 45, 60, 61, 111, 117, 119, 129, 131, 140, 141, 180, 202, 204, 205, 206, 216

McDonald's, 16, 17

Minimum Viable Product, 87, 211, 212

MVP. See Minimum Viable Product

Nielsen Norman Group, 105

North Star, 117, 124, 125, 132, 149

Old Fashioned, 82, 124

on-time in full, 59

organism, 116, 117, 119, 120, 123

OTIF. See on-time in full

outside-in, 2, 15, 19, 21, 24, 27, 37, 43, 50, 54, 56, 85, 96, 109, 113, 125, 131, 132, 171, 183, 187, 215, 218, 221, 223, 230, 231

overconfident, 62, 63, 64, 65

paint by numbers, 151, 190

PESTLE. See Political, Economic, Sociological, Technological, Legal, and Environmental

Pin the Tail on the Donkey, 23

Political, Economic, Sociological, Technological, Legal, and Environmental, 34, 35

Psychology Today, 42, 65, 72

Ready, Douglas A., 125

Reflective Competence, 88, 89, 95, 124

regression, 160

Revology, 7, 8, 10, 13, 14, 18, 21, 31, 81, 229

Rock Logic, 169, 170

Rumsfeld, Donald, 96

SaaS, 11, 12, 49, 99, 104, 105, 170

Sales, 118, 151, 228

Scarpello, Tom, 7, 14, 31, 81

SCB. See Standard Chartered Bank

self-helpy, 73

service design philosophy, 106, 108, 116

silver bullet, 27, 28, 29, 31, 32

software engineering, 9

stagnation, 30, 48, 194

stakeholders, 10, 38, 86, 108, 118, 126, 127, 135, 137, 184, 217

Standard Chartered Bank, 125

strategy, 14, 26, 28, 40, 75, 103, 137, 190, 212, 213, 217, 226, 227, 231, 234

Taco Bell, 16

tribalism, 43, 49, 50, 231

Tverskym Amos, 33

Uber Eats, 17

Uncertainty, 139

unknown knowns, 100

unknown unknowns, 96, 99, 132, 210, 222

us vs. them, 42, 49

Volatility, 139

VUCA, 139, 140, 141, 142, 144, 145, 167, 189

Walmart, 15